Boxer

AN OWNER'S GUIDE

The authors

Dr Peter Neville DHc BSc (Hons) is a Director of the Centre of Applied Pet Ethology (COAPE) group of practices, research and educational services. He has been in practice for the treatment of pet behaviour problems for over ten years. A frequent lecturer and broadcaster on pet behaviour, he is also the author of some internationally best-selling books.

Hazel Palmer MAPBC divides her time between working at the University of East London and professional pet behaviour counselling. She runs the pioneering Stratford Pet Dog Club.

Sarah Whitehead BA (Hons) is a full-time pet behaviour counsellor and a leading figure in the establishment of puppy classes and modern reward-based dog training.

David Cavill has been breeding, exhibiting, judging, photographing and writing about dogs for over twenty-five years. He is the publisher of *Dogs Monthly* and *Our Dogs and Cats* in the UK. His courses on showing, judging, breeding and animal care, which were written for the Animal Care College, are taken up by hundreds of students.

Veterinary authors

John Bower BVSc, MRCVS is a senior partner in a small animal Veterinary Hospital in Plymouth, England. He has served as President of both the British Veterinary Association and the British Small Animal Veterinary Association. He writes regularly for the veterinary press and also for dog and cat publications. He is co-author of two dog healthcare books and a member of the Kennel Club.

Caroline Bower BVM&S, MRCVS runs a veterinary health centre in the same practice as John. Her special interests include prevention and treatment of behavioural problems, and she lectures to dog breeding and training groups.

Boxer

AN OWNER'S GUIDE

Dr Peter Neville and Associates

Collir

First published in hardback in 1996 by
Collins, an imprint of
HarperCollins*Publishers*
77–85 Fulham Palace Road
Hammersmith, London W6 8JB

Reprinted 1997

The Collins website address is www.collins.co.uk

Collins is a registered trademark of HarperCollins*Publishers* Limited

This edition first published in paperback in 1999

07 06 05
 9   8   7   6

A catalogue of this book is available from the British Library

ISBN 0 00 721664 5

This book was created by SP Creative Design for HarperCollins*Publishers* Ltd
Editor: Heather Thomas
Designers: Al Rockall and Rolando Ugolini
Illustrations: Al Rockall and Rolando Ugolini
Production: Rolando Ugolini

Photography:
François Nicaise: pages 1, 6–7, 9, 11, 13, 17, 18, 21, 27, 35, 56–57, 59, 61, 62, 67, 73, 90, 92, 93-94
David Dalton: pages 3, 5, 14, 15, 22, 25, 29, 30, 32, 33, 35, 36, 37, 38, 39, 41, 43, 45, 47, 48, 49, 51, 52, 53, 54, 55, 60, 63, 64, 68, 70, 71, 73, 74, 76, 77, 79, 80, 81, 82, 83, 84, 85, 86,
Rolando Ugolini: page 91

Acknowledgments
The publishers would like to thank the following for their kind assistance in producing this book: Scampers School for Dogs for their help with photography, and special thanks to Charlie Clarricoates for all his hard work. Wendy Lunn and her dog Morris, Nadia Syphoo and her dog Tyson, Debbie Turner and her dog Harley for appearing in the special photography. Mr and Mrs K. Emerson and their dogs Islay Sersha and Starlite Skye for appearing in the photographs of the long-tailed Boxers. Annette Houldey and her Boxers Khozdar Arfer Daley and Mo for appearing in the photographs of the long-tailed Boxers.

Colour reproduction by Colourscan, Singapore
Printed and bound by Printing Express Limited, Hong Kong

CONTENTS

PART ONE – YOU AND YOUR DOG

PART TWO – CARING FOR YOUR DOG

PART THREE – HEALTHCARE

YOU AND YOUR DOG

The Boxer is one of the world's best-loved dogs
and a very popular family pet. Looking at this
fun-loving, boisterous dog, it is hard to believe that
today's Boxer is descended from mastiff-type dogs
of war and fighting dogs, which were bred
specifically for baiting bulls and bears. Although
most Boxers make good guard dogs with an effective
loud warning bark, they are renowned for their
loyalty to their owners and family and their playful
nature. They seldom 'grow up' and most never lose
their puppyish disposition, although their strength
and physical power need to be channelled into
regular exercise and stimulating games. As we
shall see, Boxers make rewarding companions and
you can have great fun training your dog and
playing with him.

CHAPTER ONE

HISTORY AND ORIGINS

BREED ORIGINS

The Boxer is one of the most popular breeds of dog kept in Europe and the United States today. Its distinctive appearance and reputation as an ideal family companion and protector have earned the Boxer its rightful place in our homes and lives.

The Boxer as a distinct breed has its beginnings at the end of the last century but its ancestry goes much further back than that to the sixteenth and seventeenth centuries when various types of dogs were used for hunting, and bull and bear baiting. These dogs, in their turn, were the descendants of the Molossis or mastiff-type dogs of war of earlier times.

In Europe, the aristocracy kept large packs of dogs for hunting wild boar and bears. These animals were chased by the lighter-built hound-types of dogs but, once cornered, they were brought down by heavier, more powerful dogs that wore protective coats of chainmail and sackcloth to protect them from the lethal tusks of boars and the slashing claws of bears. They would attack their prey, and hang on grimly until the animal became exhausted and could be killed. Many of them perished but they were extremely courageous and tenacious and would fight until the end. These powerful dogs would also have been used as watch dogs and for guarding their masters' estates.

Bull-baiting dogs

In sixteenth-century Britain, these types of dogs became the Bullenbeisser or, literally, 'bull biters', which were used in the cruel sport of attacking bulls which were tied up and unable to escape. This was relatively common in many villages, especially at local fairs and festivals, and wagers were placed on the winner of the bout.

The dogs were respected for their courage; frequently they would be shaken off by the bull, caught in the air by their owners and then thrown back into the bout. They had to be both ferocious and agile and would aim for the bull's nose and lower face and hang on grimly. To

The Boxer is an affectionate and loyal family pet with an expressive face and a highly developed sense of fun.

enable the dogs to hang on, they had undershot jaws to clamp tightly and they became very adept at fighting their large and fearsome prey. They would crouch low to avoid the bull's powerful horns, but they also had to be fit and muscular and able to twist and turn rapidly to avoid a kick from flying hooves.

The dogs used in this way for both bull and bear baiting developed a high tolerance to pain to enable them to continue to attack even when seriously wounded. They had very little loose skin around their necks, and their ears and tails were removed to prevent their victims gripping hold of them. Their

---

GUARD DOGS

It is likely that some of the early dogs to reach Great Britain were brought back by soldiers at the end of World War I. Boxers had been used as guard dogs during the war, carrying out a range of duties including guarding military sites, looking for escaped prisoners and escort work. Nowadays, dogs used by the armed services are required to disarm a suspect and then keep him at bay until their handler arrives and takes over, but in those early days Boxers were trained differently and anyone who was unwise enough to breach the security fences of army installations ran the risk not only of being stopped by the dogs but even of being killed by them.

---

very short noses would also have been advantageous to allow them to breathe during the bloody battle.

Although bull baiting was made illegal in Britain by the Humane Act of 1825 the inhumane practice was carried on in secret for many years, and these fearsome dogs were also pitted against each other in the equally cruel sport of dog fighting.

Early breed development

The first breed club, the Deutscher Boxer Club, was formed in Munich in January 1896 and held its first show in the same year. There was considerable debate among those early enthusiasts about the standard required for the breed, and the first German standard was not adopted until six years later in 1902.

The first dog to be registered in the newly formed stud book was a dog called Flocki. Born in 1895, he was also the first Boxer to be shown. Flocki's sire was a white English Bulldog from Munich, although in those days the bulldog looked vastly different from those of today, being lighter and taller.

The number of Boxers increased rapidly until the outbreak of World War I. Breeding was closely controlled in those early days; breed wardens would decide on the suitability of particular animals for mating to conform to the standard, and there was considerable close line and

inbreeding to establish type. Many of the early dogs were white or patched with other colours, and it was some years before the uniformity of colours that we recognise today was established. These controls on breeding are still very much to the fore in Germany today, and dogs must also be tested to show their courage before they are used in breeding programmes. This is to ensure that the particular characteristics, temperament and physical appearance of the breed will survive for future generations.

The pedigrees of most modern Boxers can be traced back to the dogs of the Stockmanns' von Dom kennels, which were established in the early part of this century. Their dogs were a major

With his powerful, muscular physique, the Boxer is a large, active dog with a friendly nature.

influence on the breed. In fact, Frau Stockmann was an artist and through her drawings she has left the breeders of today a legacy of the appearance of those early dogs.

Early breed enthusiasts

The British Boxer Club was established in 1936 and the first British champion was a dog called Horsa of Leith Hill who gained his title in 1939. Today's owners will probably never appreciate the many difficulties that those early breed enthusiasts in Germany and Great

Britain went through to keep their lines going through World War II when it would have been difficult to ensure the survival of their own families without the additional problems of finding enough food for their dogs.

FAMOUS CHAMPIONS

There were many dogs of the post-war years that were of significant importance to the breed's development, including Ch. Seefeld Picasso, a top show dog of the 1960s who sired eighteen UK champions. Other famous names that may be found in the pedigrees of today's Boxers include Ch. Marbelton Desperate Dan and, more recently, Ch. Tyegarth Famous Grouse. One show-winning dog, Ch. Seefield Holbein, even achieved a title in a working trial, demonstrating the Boxer's versatility.

After the war ended it took some years to re-establish and build up breeding programmes, and the numbers of dogs registered with the Kennel Club grew quite slowly, reaching 707 in 1946. However, there was a rapid expansion over the next decade, as with other breeds in the post-war years, and many Boxers were imported into Britain from Europe and the United States.

Before 1945, ownership of pedigree dogs was not a standard part of family life, particularly in urban areas, unless people had a particular interest in a specific breed and its development, or the dog was being used for a job of work. Our attitude to owning dogs in general, and particularly pedigree dogs, has changed greatly and now pedigree dogs are more numerous as pets than the mongrel or cross-breed.

THE KENNEL CLUB BREED STANDARD

Reproduced with kind permission of the Kennel Club

General Appearance Great nobility, smooth-coated, medium-sized, square build, strong bone and evident, well developed muscles.

Characteristics Lively, strong, loyal to owner and family, but distrustful of strangers. Obedient, friendly at play, but with guarding instinct.

Temperament Equable, biddable, fearless, self-assured.

Head and Skull Head imparts its unique individual stamp and is in proportion to body, appearing neither light nor too heavy. Skull lean without exaggerated cheek muscles. Muzzle broad, deep and powerful, never narrow, pointed, short or shallow. Balance of skull and muzzle essential, with muzzle never appearing small, viewed from any angle. Skull cleanly covered, showing no wrinkle, except when alerted. Creases present from root of nose running down sides of muzzle. Dark mask confined to muzzle, distinctly contrasting with colour of head, even when white is present. Lower jaw undershot, curving slightly upward. Upper jaw broad where attached to skull, tapering very slightly to front. Muzzle shape completed by upper lips, thick and well padded, supported by well separated canine teeth of lower jaw. Lower edge of upper lip rests on edge of lower lip, so that chin is clearly perceptible when viewed from front or side. Lower jaw never to obscure front of upper lip, neither should teeth nor tongue be visible when mouth closed. Top of skull slightly arched, not rounded, nor too flat and broad. Occiput not too pronounced. Distinct stop, bridge of nose never forced back into forehead, nor should it be downfaced. Length of muzzle measured from tip of nose to inside corner of eye is one-third length of head measured from tip of nose to occiput. Nose broad, black, slightly turned up, wide nostrils with well defined line between. Tip of nose set slightly higher than root of muzzle. Cheeks powerfully developed, never bulging.

THE BREED STANDARD

Size Height: dogs: 57-63 cms (22 1/2-25 ins); bitches: 53-59 cms (21-23 ins). Weight: dogs: approximately 30-32 kgs (66-70 lbs); bitches: approximately 25-27 kgs (55-60lbs).

Colour Fawn or brindle. White markings acceptable not exceeding one-third of ground colour.
Fawn: Various shades from dark deer red to light fawn.
Brindle: Black stripes on previously described fawn shades, running parallel to ribs all over body. Stripes contrast distinctly to ground colour, neither too close nor too thinly dispersed. Ground colour clear, not intermingling with stripes.

Tail Set on high, customarily docked and carried upward.

Hindquarters Very strong with muscles hard and standing out noticeably under skin. Thighs broad and curved. Broad croup slightly sloped, with flat, broad arch. Pelvis long and broad. Upper and lower thigh long. Good hind angulation; when standing, the stifle is directly under the hip protuberance. Seen from side, leg from hock joint to foot not quite vertical. Seen from behind, legs straight, hock joints clean, with powerful rear pads.

Body In profile square, length from forechest to rear of upper thigh equal to height at withers. Chest deep, reaching to elbows. Depth of chest half height at withers. Ribs well arched, not barrel-shaped, extending well to rear. Withers clearly defined. Back short, straight, slightly sloping, broad and strongly muscled. Loin short, well tucked up and taut. Lower abdominal line blends into curve to rear.

Note Male animals should have two apparently normal testicles fully descended into the scrotum.

Coat Short, glossy, smooth and tight to body.

Feet Front feet small and cat-like, with well-arched toes, and hard pads; hind feet slightly longer.

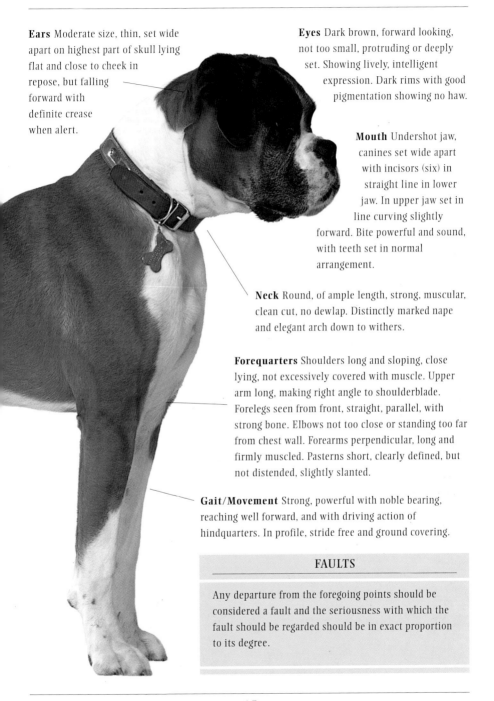

Ears Moderate size, thin, set wide apart on highest part of skull lying flat and close to cheek in repose, but falling forward with definite crease when alert.

Eyes Dark brown, forward looking, not too small, protruding or deeply set. Showing lively, intelligent expression. Dark rims with good pigmentation showing no haw.

Mouth Undershot jaw, canines set wide apart with incisors (six) in straight line in lower jaw. In upper jaw set in line curving slightly forward. Bite powerful and sound, with teeth set in normal arrangement.

Neck Round, of ample length, strong, muscular, clean cut, no dewlap. Distinctly marked nape and elegant arch down to withers.

Forequarters Shoulders long and sloping, close lying, not excessively covered with muscle. Upper arm long, making right angle to shoulderblade. Forelegs seen from front, straight, parallel, with strong bone. Elbows not too close or standing too far from chest wall. Forearms perpendicular, long and firmly muscled. Pasterns short, clearly defined, but not distended, slightly slanted.

Gait/Movement Strong, powerful with noble bearing, reaching well forward, and with driving action of hindquarters. In profile, stride free and ground covering.

FAULTS

Any departure from the foregoing points should be considered a fault and the seriousness with which the fault should be regarded should be in exact proportion to its degree.

CHARACTERISTICS

The Boxer is a very loyal and loving companion within the family but can be suspicious of strangers. This trait develops as the dog approaches maturity and is seen more commonly in males than females. Faithful and affectionate, the Boxer is an effective guard dog, although he will not bark without reason.

The ideal Boxer will stand erect and alert against any possible threat, and most of us are accustomed to the sight of a determined and confident dog behind his garden gate! He will adopt a dominant stance and will position himself between the potential intruder and his owner or property. Prospective owners must be aware of this trait in order to avoid potential problems and should never encourage or torment the dog to demonstrate this guarding behaviour. As with any dog, a Boxer should never show aggression to visitors, and this protective element of his nature should be borne in mind. Owners should ensure that they are the 'leader of the pack' and are in control of their dog in every situation.

Lifespan

The Boxer is a very slow maturing breed and will remain playful and active. However, it is not a particularly long-lived breed, with ten years being a good age for most dogs. They may be described as having an adolescent mentality for years and then becoming elderly almost overnight; they do not slow down gracefully nor do they have a drawn-out middle age.

Companionship

Boxers become very attached to their family and are not really suited to being left alone for hours at a time while their owners are at work. They become very attached to their owners and thrive on companionship, and can become unhappy when left for long periods. Indeed, they can be extremely destructive and many owners can vouch for the power in those jaws when they divert their attention to carpets or furniture if they are bored or lonely. Owners must therefore be prepared to include their Boxer in as many areas of their lives as possible. As puppies, they will require consistency in their training to ensure that they develop into sociable adults, both with people and other animals.

Strength and fitness

In play, Boxers have frequent exhaustive bouts of activity, and as puppies and adolescents they often use their body

EXERCISE

Boxers enjoy exercise and activity and will be instantly ready for a walk whatever the weather. Prospective owners must be prepared for this and should allow adequate time to give their dog regular daily exercise, and also set aside some time during the day and evening to interact with their Boxer by playing games and training him. They are not the breed for someone who wants a dog that curls up by the fire. A Boxer is an intelligent, boisterous and active dog, who requires both physical exercise and mental stimulation for his well-being. If these are not provided, then some problems are almost guaranteed to arise.

strength and flexibility to 'wrestle' with other dogs. They have a habit of standing on their hind legs and using their front paws against another dog in play; this is reminiscent of a boxing bout and it has led to speculation that this is the origin of their name. If reared and exercised correctly, the Boxer will become an extremely fit and muscular dog and care should be taken that garden fences are high enough to contain him.

Family pets

Boxers have a reputation for being good with children but they are not always suitable for a family with very young children or toddlers. As with any medium-sized, active breed, they tend to move around a lot and can knock over a young child accidentally. Due to their love of play they are likely to see young children as ideal partners in games and can become over-boisterous.

They are perhaps more suited to families with older children who can be taught to assist in training the puppy from an early age so that play does not get out of control. It should be remembered that an adult Boxer is a large and powerful dog and should never be walked alone by young children. Parents must be prepared to supervise any activity, either play or exercise, in which dogs and children are interacting. They should also take into account the protective

nature of the Boxer, particularly if their child invites friends into the home. Normal play between children can be riotous and noisy, and a dog of any of the companion/guard breeds may perceive this play as a physical assault on a young member of 'his' pack and could become over-protective.

Expressive behaviour

Boxers seem to have a highly developed sense of fun which is almost unique among dogs and appear to thoroughly enjoy acting the 'clown'. They will often

The Boxer's highly expressive face makes him very appealing.

develop a repertoire of comic behaviours which will be quickly adopted if they are reinforced by laughter from their adoring audience. Sometimes they even appear to check that everyone is paying attention before performing their 'party piece'.

A Boxer also has a very expressive face and his owner will quickly learn to interpret every wrinkling of his nose or movement of his ears, or is it that we can more easily interpret the moods and intentions of a flat-faced dog because it resembles our own more closely than the long-muzzled faces of German Shepherds and many other favourite breeds.

Aggression in male dogs and communication

As with any male dog, male Boxers can sometimes develop aggression problems with other male dogs and this should be considered when buying a puppy, particularly if you live in an urban area where the dog will frequently be exercised in parks or playing fields in close proximity with many other dogs. In common with male dogs of many breeds, Boxers may become territorial in the areas where they are walked regularly and react aggressively towards other males whom they may view as invading their territory.

This characteristic does not develop until the dog is mature but many owners are shocked when their playful male adolescent suddenly becomes the local canine 'lager lout'! Boxers will not necessarily be the instigator of a fight but they will certainly not back down once a problem arises. If this happens several times then it may become a learned behaviour and the dog may actively go looking for trouble.

One of the problems that a male Boxer may have in canine communication is that the breed has a natural, very upright, dominant body posture, which may have been made more pronounced by the docked tail, which has been part of the breed's appearance until recently. This body stance may be quite provocative to other dominant males who may then challenge him.

Another factor in the reaction of other dogs to Boxers is that they may not always find the Boxer's facial and body expressions easy to read and consequently may be quite wary. In addition, the Boxer's noisy breathing may be perceived as a threat by other dogs and thus the young Boxer may find himself in trouble through no fault of his own. To avoid this, owners should socialize their Boxer puppy with as many different dogs as possible to enable him to develop those 'canine social skills' that he will require when he is older.

Saliva

Although breeding today for modern conformation as required by Kennel Club standards means that Boxers' mouths should not sag, they frequently do produce a slobbery saliva which their owners are accustomed to removing from clothes and furniture. This is only a minor point but it should be taken into account by any prospective owner who is particularly houseproud and who should maybe look for a more suitable breed.

CHAPTER TWO

BEHAVIOUR AND TRAINING

THE DEVELOPMENT OF DOGS

The playful, powerful, fearless and friendly Boxer is one of our most distinctive, easily recognisable and loved breeds of dog, be he brindle, fawn, red or white. But how did he evolve and why does he look and behave so differently to the ancestor of all dogs, the wolf? And how, when he was originally developed as a hunter, fighter and guard, does the Boxer now make such a great pet for the modern active family?

The man/dog relationship began in the Mesolithic period about 10,000 to 14,000 years ago and progressed with little change until the twentieth century. Until then man had predominantly bred Boxers and all dogs for what they did and not for how they looked. However, in the last hundred years or so, there has been a shift of emphasis away from the selection of a dog's ability to perform particular tasks to one based on how a dog looks and its social temperament. This has been caused by the massive rise in ownership of dogs kept purely as pets with little or no obligation to work or contribute to the family pack other than as companions. In the past fifty years or so especially, our expectations of what dogs should look like and how they should behave have altered enormously and this shift in emphasis probably lies at the root of many of the physical and behavioural problems now seen in many of our modern breeds of dog.

However, the playful, boisterous Boxer, like so many of the flatter-faced (or brachycephalic) breeds, seems to have made the change from his main role as hunting partner and fighting dog to that of family companion with fewer psychological problems at least than many other breeds, even if, physically, his flat face has given him a little more to contend with than many others.

Evolution of the dog

Recent research has shown that different breeds of dog organise their social

Boxers come in a wide range of colours, including brindle, fawn and red.

structure in different ways, i.e. what is important to one breed, in terms of 'pack rules' and communication systems, is unimportant to another. For example, some breeds, such as the Husky, are sensitive to which member of their group is given attention first by a visiting stranger. If a dog of a lower rank is privileged by being given attention, a great deal of tension may develop between the other dogs in the group.

Dogs of some other breeds do not seem to care which member of their group is greeted first; instead, they seem to place great importance on the possession of a new toy. Other breeds may value access to the food bowl while Boxers may organise their social relations more around physical access to members of their family group who provide them with security and affection.

A process of selection

A study in the United States questioned why, if all dogs have evolved from an efficient predator like the wolf, livestock-guarding breeds are so much less likely to kill their charges than most other breeds, whereas others, e.g. the Greyhound,

Like all other breeds of dog, the Boxer evolved from the wolf.

SURVIVAL IN A CHANGING ENVIRONMENT

The three survival imperatives for any animal are:

- Feeding
- Reproducing
- Staying out of trouble

Physical changes in an animal are triggered by changes in the environment, and its behavioural adaptations to ensure survival. The change in the environment that facilitated the domestication of the wolf into the dog occurred when man began to adopt a village way of life. This provided a year-round stable food supply for wild animals if they could move in near enough to him to exploit it. The rubbish dumps just outside early man's villages and settlements would have provided a good source of scavengeable food for wolves and would have been used as a safe place for adult wolves to leave the juveniles while they were out hunting. Although past the very dependent cub stage and out of the den, these juveniles would not yet be sufficiently old or experienced enough to join the hunt. Dumps would have been an ideal place to leave them as all the other predators, such as large cats, were mainly solitary and would have been less likely to approach man's settlements in order to pursue them.

retain strong predatory instincts.

The scientists concluded that the manipulation of the wolf's genes that occurred in the process of domestication to create the great variety of differently behaved dogs that we know today, could not have begun with early man capturing and somehow taming a predatory adult wolf. Nor could it have begun with man hand-rearing a wolf cub, because even if he could have got close enough to a wolf den to take one, he would not have had the knowledge nor the ability to wean it properly. Furthermore, even if he found or took a cub and tried to wean it, it would have grown up into an adult wolf, complete with potentially dangerous predatory instincts, albeit perhaps maintained with a sociable attitude towards man, as can be observed today when wolves, coyotes and foxes are hand-reared and maintain human contact as adults. All dogs, including the Bulldog and the Bullenbeisser breeds that contributed to the development of the Boxer, must therefore have evolved from the wolf through a much more subtle process of selection than one actively dictated by man.

Domesticating the wolf

The wolves that benefited most from the stable food supply and security of the rubbish dumps (see box above) were those that learned to live and survive close to man without running away. The bolder juveniles would soon have become sufficiently confident to enter the village to scavenge on the richer resources of the waste in the streets and on the contents of latrines. All of this biodegradable waste was of no use to man in his village, but it could be utilized by dogs and converted into canine protein for humans to eat.

Probably, man could not have chased the young wolves away even if he had wanted to, but there was an ulterior motive for him to want them around. His switch from being a hunter/gatherer to a crop-farming way of life would have made an easily obtainable year-round meat supply highly advantageous. Juicy young wolves would have fitted the menu nicely, and therefore it would have been in man's interests to tolerate their scavenging activities.

Once a resident population of young wolves was established in the village and had stayed to reach maturity and breed there, man would soon have become aware of which wolf/dogs produced the biggest and fattest puppies and encouraged them for eating later. Direct physical contact, taming and socialization of village-born puppies

EARLY TYPES OF DOG

Early man encouraged the village dogs indirectly to grow up retaining the playful characteristics of juvenile wolves, and not to develop the full range of social behaviour or the predatory behaviours typical of adult wolves. In this way, man could accept them without any danger to himself. These characteristics became established in the adult, reproductive population of village dogs, but there were some differences.

■ **Hunting dogs**
Some dogs would have retained near-adult qualities in terms of their predatory behaviour patterns and they would have been ideal for helping man to stalk his prey when he went out to hunt.

■ **Herding dogs**
Hunting dogs would also have been useful in helping man to herd his sheep and other livestock outside the village, but only once the bite/kill end of the hunting sequence (see page 26) had been selected out by man, who would have culled any dogs that attacked his livestock, or would have used them for hunting instead.

■ **Livestock guarding dogs**
Dogs that remained very juvenile in their behaviour and showed no propensity to hunt or herd would have been ideal for guarding livestock.

■ **Retrieving dogs**
The slightly more adult types of dog would have developed possessive instincts over objects and these would have been selected for by man in order to train them to use as retrievers on the hunt.

BREEDS OF DOG

We might conclude from this that there was no such thing as a breed of dog, because breeds are man-made; there is only a type of dog. This may seem contradictory to the earlier idea that breeds of dog vary so much in their behaviour that each one should be considered as an individual form. However, the different types of dog originally arose because of their different inherent behaviour traits. Nowadays the various breeds demonstrate different behaviour traits to enable them to co-exist and co-operate with each other. Therefore, both ideas are accurate. What is certain is that the full combined expression of adult social and predatory behaviours of the wolf, the ancestor of all dogs, is not seen in any type or breed of domestic dog, including the Boxer.

with man would then have occurred as a crucial part of the domestication process.

Breeding for behaviour

Dogs that performed well at what they were expected to do would have been kept and bred from, and their skills refined in most cases through specific types of training, while others that were not so good would probably have been killed and eaten. At this stage, and for the following thousands of years, man did not care about his dog's appearance; he was only interested in its behaviour. Dogs were bred for their behavioural characteristics and it was man's selection for these attributes that encouraged the different types to evolve.

BEHAVIOUR VERSUS TEMPERAMENT

Many pedigree dogs (including the Boxer) were bred originally to perform tasks that were far removed from the largely indoor lives they now lead. Paradoxically, if behavioural changes in dog types are so inherently and originally linked to physical changes, then selecting primarily for appearance as practised in the show world today must inevitably destabilize the predictability of the behaviour of all types of dogs.

We should not be surprised that so many dogs develop behaviour problems when bred and kept mainly for their appearance rather than selecting for the ability to do the job that originally made them the way they look. Nor that there are now so many canine psychologists in practice to help them cope with their new lifestyles, and dogs and their owners to cope with each other!

Some canine psychologists interpret 'behaviour' as the expression of what a dog has been physically and genetically programmed to do, whereas 'temperament' is considered to be an emotional response which dictates how it utilizes these programmed skills. 'Good temperament' in a pet dog usually means that it is friendly with other dogs and people, especially children. Therefore it is measured more by considerations of its sociability rather than its working behaviour.

THE PREDATORY SEQUENCE

All wild hunters, including wolves, must develop and learn to co-ordinate the necessary sensory abilities and instinctive physical skills when young in order to complete this predatory sequence of behaviour as adults: Detect (see/scent/hear) – Eye – Follow – Stalk – Chase – Grasp/Bite – Kill.

Note: if this sequence is interrupted at any stage, the predator must start the hunt again from the beginning by getting a new fix on the position of his quarry. This sequence was truncated through selection of juvenile characteristics in the early dogs so that the full adult sequences of hunting were inhibited at various stages.

Instinct versus temperament

The Boxer also was originally and specifically developed as a hunter type, but by a deliberate cross-breeding of two hunter/fighter types, the Bulldog and the powerful German Bullenbeisser. The Boxer was 'manufactured' as a strong fearless type with a high pain threshold so that it could be employed to hunt and bring down large and dangerous game, e.g. bears and wild boar, which the traditional

hunting Greyhound types might chase but fear to approach at the end of the hunt.

However, as well as selecting for strength and fearlessness in Boxers, man also selected for a rather juvenile character in their social behaviour to make their strength and power safe and manageable around us. This has manifested in a character that, like a child, is easily distracted at any time and so is less likely to concentrate for long enough on 'prey' to be able to develop a predatory sequence of behaviour in the same way as a Greyhound.

The Boxer's predatory behaviour was originally focused through deliberate selection of dogs that, while unlikely to begin or advance through the normal early parts of the sequence of eye/stalk/chase in their normal disposition that

Boxers have boundless energy and enjoy physical exercise.

Greyhounds and herding dogs will readily express, nonetheless quickly and powerfully complete the final stages of 'grasp/bite/kill'. This meant that Boxers could be safely 'wound up' and excited through encouragement by their handlers to be 'set upon' their quarry once it was in view. This capacity for intense, directed violent aggression quickly resulted in Boxers being employed to bait and attack such animals as bears, bulls or even other dogs in the 'sport pits' of the time. These horrendous 'sports' are now hopefully gone for ever, and we select our fighting breeds of old more for the wonderful social juvenile side of their character.

In spite of this, Boxers and Bull

Terriers are still relatively easy to train to display the aggressive behaviour that was originally prized in their make-up. On occasion, they can also learn to employ aggression for themselves to deal with threats and challenges and discover that their inherited strength, power and seeming imperviousness to pain enable them to survive. If they then go on to use that aggression instantly to control less threatening situations, e.g. in minor social disputes with other dogs, they can be difficult and dangerous dogs to treat. Thankfully, our continued selection for their friendly tolerant nature helps to ensure that such problems are rare.

The Boxer in the human pack

The attributes needed for a good hunting dog are not only a controllable sequence of predatory behaviour, but also a willingness to accept our interruption of that behaviour and a control of all our social interactions through being socially appeasing. Then even hunter/fighter types such as the Boxer quickly become attractive to us as safe social companions albeit with something of an 'edge'.

A dog that was good at the Boxer's original tasks of the close-quarter elements of hunting, fighting and baiting, if it survived, would have enjoyed long years of working partnership with its owner, and may well have been used for breeding to pass on its attributes.

Selection for appearance

Selection based mainly on performance at a 'job' causes certain physical attributes to be maintained in any type of dog, most notably muscular strength and stamina in the Boxer. However, such features are less likely to be maintained once any type is selected primarily for sociability with people, or when a breed is selected mainly for the degree to which the individuals conform to the changing fads of the human view of ideal appearance in the dog show ring.

As a result, smaller, slimmer and less robust-looking Boxers soon arose and now predominate, with far less chance of expressing the hunting/fighting behaviours for which they were originally developed. These new types of dog have found favour in the show dog world simply for their physical appearance.

Boxers as pets

In the past, a dog that was not so good at its 'work' tended to be destroyed and replaced with a 'good one', irrespective of how it looked. However, if it was lucky, the 'not-so-good' worker was found a home as a non-working pet, where its friendly character served it and its new owners well, even if its bravery, fighting skills and robust physical attributes were less vital for the new 'job'. It is as one of the most popular breeds of pet dog perhaps that Boxers are most loved

DEALING WITH THREATS AND CHALLENGES – 'THE FOUR F'S'

Aggression is one of the four strategies for coping with the fear of threats and challenges. It is the 'fight' response, with 'flight' (running away), 'freeze' (and hope to go unnoticed) and 'fiddle about' (appease) being the other alternatives. Most dogs are more likely to adopt 'fiddle about' as their coping strategy in a social conflict with their owners or with other familiar people and dogs, but large reactive types, such as Boxers, originally developed specifically as hunters and then fighters, and nowadays often kept as guards, can learn to adopt 'fight'. This may be a successful policy for them on some occasions and we may even encourage and school such responses, e.g. when Boxers are trained as some are in mainland Europe and elsewhere for some aspects of duty with the police and armed forces. In a more domestic setting, if such a strategy becomes adopted and employed by the dog to help it deal with everyday events that are not genuinely physically challenging or threatening, such as the arrival of visitors to the family home, it can quickly lead to many difficult problems of 'aggression' that require careful attention to be overcome successfully.

nowadays. Their enormously attractive, large, strong appearance and human-like flat face appeals very strongly to our desire to keep the image of a muscular, protective 'wolf' in our living room, and gives us the idea that we can still enjoy regular contact with the wild side of nature. Their dependency on living in a social group brings an associated loyalty to us and a willingness to protect us against threats and to defend our shared den. The Boxer's ever-willing desire to get involved with us in every activity makes him extremely attractive as a pet.

Understanding working type

An understanding of a particular breed's original working type should be a priority for the owner of any dog, as well as for the dog trainer or canine behaviourist. In the process of selecting for working type in most of our dogs, we have deliberately excluded dogs that in a social conflict showed a tendency to select 'fight' as their coping strategy (see page 29).

Later, such qualities were thought desirable for certain tasks in some types such as Boxers and their immediate contributory forebears, and dogs were selected that would adopt 'fight' as their coping strategy but with a more controllable edge as a result of their domesticated willingness to be socially appeasing. These types of dog would have been the forerunners of Boxers and many other breeds that are recognised nowadays as being primarily guarding dogs. In their case, the 'fight' strategy has been harnessed and usually directed at challenges outside the dog's immediate pack or social group. The Boxer is so attractive as a friendly but protective pet because of his:

- Physical size and strength.
- Willingness to be socially appeasing ('fiddle about') to resolve conflicts with members of his own social group.

The more you invest in developing a friendly, social relationship with your Boxer, the more you'll get out of owning one. The protective behaviour will usually appear naturally as an added bonus once he is older in the form of a good loud guarding bark from a large dog which will deter most would-be burglars without the need for any attacks.

HOW DOGS COMMUNICATE

The development of language has arisen out of the need for some animals to communicate with each other in order to survive, both in finding a mate and, in animals such as wolves, in developing the necessary co-operative social skills needed to hunt and protect shared resources of food, shelter and breeding areas together. In this way, each individual and the genes of the species benefit from a shared approach. The complexity and nature of language determine how successful any animal can be socially with its own kind. Expression of emotions, direction and intention by one animal and their interpretation by another and subsequent organisation of responses enables each to predict the behaviour of the other and thus contribute to their combined success.

Communicating mood

When signalling an assertive mood or intent on a social encounter, the wolf or dog stands upright with his tail usually held high and perhaps arched over his back. The Boxer was one of the breeds whose tail was traditionally docked in a practice now outlawed in the UK and some other European countries, so this form of communication was not available to him. Thankfully, he will now be able

WHAT IS LANGUAGE?

In most social mammals, communication takes three major forms of direct language:
- Vocal signals
- Body/facial movements
- Touch

Dogs, and most other animals that live in co-operative groups, largely learn the direct language skills demanded for such a social lifestyle between the ages of weaning and the onset of sexual maturity, schooled under the protective supervision of their parents and other older members of the group into which they are destined to integrate.

Dogs and wolves have many of their communication methods in common and show similar facial and body postures, especially with regard to establishing relative status and in communicating emotional states, such as aggression and fear. The position of the ears, the degree of opening of the eyes and the direction of stare, and the opening of the mouth and display of teeth are all used to help signal anxiety, excitement, fear or invitation to approach and play, and also to help communicate an enormous range of moods expressed by dogs, one to another.

to signal his emotions like most other dogs, with the long whippy tail that nature provided for him.

Signalling assertion

The assertive wolf or dog also signals his mood by holding his head up with ears erect to convey a message of being large and powerful. Sadly, ear cropping to make the ears permanently erect has also long been practised in many countries to enhance the Boxer's assertive appearance, although this has been illegal in the UK for many years. This, too, may have ensured that Boxers have often given off inadvertently the wrong signals to other dogs in social encounters and perhaps found themselves in trouble as a result.

Signalling submission

A wolf signalling subordination in a social encounter can communicate fully and may drop its body and keep its head below the level of its back with its ears flattened. The tail is held low and may wag at the end, all of these signals being designed to deflect a social threat and appease a more assertive animal in any particular conflict. Additionally, a submissive dog may also withdraw its lips and 'grin' as it approaches a higher-ranking packmate, often in association with other body language signs of submission, but this is virtually impossible for a Boxer because of its flattened face and level or undershot lower jaw. A dramatic, and perhaps last-resort, communication of passive submission is shown when a dog rolls on its back and presents its underbelly, a posture that *in extremis* was still available to the docked, cropped, undershot Boxer who was trying to signal compliance or subordination.

Signals for resolving conflicts

All of the signals described above are designed to communicate moods and intentions in an effort to resolve conflicts without having to resort to physical violence. It is, after all, not in either party's interests to injure a fellow packmate, as injuring even the lowest-ranking member may weaken the survival prospects of every other member and thereby threaten the survival chances of the co-operative group.

To avoid such a prospect in, for example, a social greeting ritual between packmates after a period of separation, the established subordinate dog of a pair will usually break eye contact from its higher-ranking colleague as a gesture of appeasement and acceptance and thereby help to reaffirm their respective social relationships without conflict.

This is why your dog may attempt to avoid eye contact with you and may appear confused and even frightened if you persist in staring at him.

Communication via scent

Many animals, including dogs, also communicate using the indirect language of visual marks and pheromones – the chemical messengers of scent. Domestic dogs rely more on communication via scent than we can really appreciate with our very poor sense of smell.

Scent marking enables signals to remain in the environment for longer periods than direct forms of language and can impart a message after a dog has left a particular area. Scent signals used in the marking of territory include the deposition of faeces, urine and glandular secretions, which give an individual signature odour to each and every dog.

VOCAL COMMUNICATION

It is vocal signals that enable dogs to communicate over long distances and in situations where visual signals are inefficient; for example, at night or in dense cover. Additionally, hearing a bark or a howl enables a dog to pin-point at a distance where the other dog is at the precise time of the signal, and so react to it immediately.

Barking, growling and howling

Dogs trace their evolution from the wolf at the one time of its development when it is quite noisy and makes sounds similar to barks – the juvenile phase. Probably as a direct result of this, adult dogs bark far more than adult wolves and can develop a wide repertoire of vocal signals. Barks are used in defence of territory, in play and as an attention-seeking language in greeting, whereas low growls are used as warning and threat signals in social altercations, and a higher range of whimpers, whines and yips is used to deflect social challenges, and in excitable greetings.

Wolves howl to maintain contact with other members when physically isolated and unable to use direct language, and to rally the pack when hunting. Dogs, with the exception of the chasing hounds, howl primarily as a signal of anxiety, notably when left alone

by their owners. Some breeds are noisier than others, and Boxers are above average when it comes to barking, with the ability and readiness to sound a very loud, deep bark as required when they are guarding the home or car.

Communicating your leadership

The ability to form a social bond with people is not exclusive to the dog in the canid family. For example, hand-raised wolves and coyotes can be extremely sociable with their handlers, yet they differ from dogs in the level of distress experienced when they are isolated from them.

Dogs show much more distress when separated from their humans, a dependency that underlines the 'perpetual juvenile' theory very nicely. Your dog views you perhaps somewhere between a parental figure and a packmate, from whom to expect signals of leadership and protection. Since you are also the packmate who provides food, initiates hunting excursions (walks) and play, defines sleeping areas and initiates many of your social interactions, your role as director is regularly reinforced. A stable leader does not maintain his position by a regime of force, threat and punishment, but through communicating his strengths, will and moods effectively and safely to members of his group so that his right to lead is accorded to him by them.

Understanding the social structure of a pack animal is relatively simple – the higher up the ladder you are, the more privileges you are granted, but when dogs live in a mixed pack containing humans, dogs (perhaps of different types) and cats, understanding the rules can become confusing. As humans, we attempt to teach the dog many of our values and expect him to understand our methods of communication, but the dog is only capable of learning via languages that he can interpret and can only understand canine values. These vary enormously between types, breeds, gender and the nature of individual dogs.

The leader of the pack

Different breeds and types of dog organise their social structure in different ways, suggesting that there is a need for some to organise a social system both between themselves and with their human pack-mates. Some breeds seem to be rather unconcerned about having a leader of their pack, or alpha figure, but most, including Boxers, seem to expect to live in a group with a leader or even several parental figures. In any case, we normally expect to manage and dictate the dog's behaviour and lifestyle and so effectively appoint ourselves as leader and expect him to learn how to respond to our direction.

Some dogs begin to regard the acquisition of control of certain aspects of their lives with us as indicating a high rank in their pack and may start to take advantage of their position and become difficult to manage. The simple procedures described here, once accepted by your opportunist dog, will help ensure that he will respond more willingly to being trained, once he has learned the meaning of your training signals, because he respects your superior rank.

A professional pet behaviour counsellor will be able to help structure the application of these non-confrontational ideas to treat specific behaviour problems in a dog, but these suggestions can be used at any time to ensure that your dog views his position within your pack as secure and lower ranking than you and your family, and to establish your right to direct his actions.

1 Freedom of movement It is the right of the high-ranking members of your pack, i.e. you and your family, to move about your shared den and rest and sleep where you wish. Try to deny your dog similar freedom of movement around the house, and make upstairs, the centre of the den where you sleep, a 'no go' area for him. This can be achieved by keeping some downstairs doors shut to keep him out of certain rooms for a few days until he accepts his new restricted access, and by fitting a baby gate at the bottom of the stairs.

By the same token, try not to allow the dog on your chairs and define his main sleeping area, at least, as one secure comfortable bed on the floor which you can remove or occupy if you wish. Remember that height reinforces social rank and comfortable resting places might be worth competing for, so try to prevent possible conflict and don't put him in an artificially high-ranking position by giving him your privileges of unopposed movement throughout the den and free access to your resting areas.

2 **Social interaction** Make sure that all the benefits of social interaction for your dog, e.g. being stroked, fed, given treats, walked and played with, are usually initiated by you rather than your dog obtaining them on demand. In some cases, the dog is continually dictating the order of your social relationship, deciding who is going to stroke him, when he will be stroked and for how long the interaction will continue. Calling him to you and asking him to sit and wait before stroking him puts you back in control without reducing the total time spent in contact, or the quality of your relationship.

This restructuring of the mutual relationship and earning of desirable aspects of contact will communicate very quickly that you are the higher-ranking animal and that it is worth your dog's while to wait for your signals. He should then learn consistently to approach you a little more cautiously and 'politely' when wanting affection or other rewarding contact, and then you will be able to respond to his modified approach without any risk of elevating his status to the point where he wishes to dictate the order of life to you again.

3 **Feeding** Top dogs usually eat first and subordinates must wait until the food source is vacated before gaining access, so it can sometimes help to prepare your dog's meals in his presence and then make him wait for them while you eat. This may seem like teasing, especially to a ravenous puppy, but it instinctively tells him that at feeding times you get the best first; he gets the rest when you allow him access to his food bowl. This is especially important with puppies and young dogs as, weight for weight, they need to take in a lot more food relative to adult dogs in order to grow. As they are

always hungry they can be taught new commands and come to accept their social position very easily by manipulating the availability of food.

4 **Strength games** When young, most types of dog use possession of trophies to instigate ritualized forms of competition to help define their relative strength and handling skills and develop social relations with each other. Some dogs, such as retriever types, invariably continue to use possession of objects and toys as the main method of maintaining their social order as adults. 'Those who play together, stay together!' But

it can sometimes be important only to play competitive strength games, such as tug-o-war, if you are prepared to win them, and this can be very difficult with a powerful dog such as the Boxer.

'Winning' means that you must end up ultimately with the tug toy and keep possession by putting it somewhere out of the dog's reach, so if you can't win when you wish, don't play this type of game with a Boxer. Remember that he has a strong jaw grip and can be very tough in competition! All such games are, in any case, best played outdoors where they have less social significance and perhaps are more concerned with the development of co-ordinated hunting skills than social competition.

5 **Follow the leader** Try to make sure that you usually go through narrow openings, e.g. doorways and passageways, first and effectively lead

MOTIVATIONAL TOYS

The best games for a dog to play alone focus on encouraging the natural behaviours that stimulate mental and physical activity. The Buster Cube is an excellent motivational toy, and is recommended by canine behaviourists, trainers and vets. It can be filled with dry food kibbles and given to the dog who must nose and paw it around in order to make the food appear. This will make him think and employ his natural foraging skills to obtain the food, keeping him positively occupied, especially when he has to be left alone.

your dog through. Encourage him to follow you, not lead or herd you through an open doorway. If he tries to push ahead, shut the door gently and block his path, repeating the procedure until he hesitates and allows you to move through unopposed.

6 **Rights of passage** Expect your dog to move out of your way when you move about the house – fitting a light

trailing house line to the collar or Gentle Leader headcollar system (see page 46) for a few days allows you to do this easily. Call your dog to come to you when you need him and always encourage him to move towards you for contact or attention rather than going humbly to him.

Creating effective communication

Of course, there are thousands of pet dogs who are being afforded some or all of these signals of authority on a daily basis, but they do not present a problem. They are perfectly biddable either because, like the Boxer, they are not particularly status conscious, or the hundreds of other signals that you give convey that you are 'in charge'.

If your dog is not a problem in his control, training or behaviour and he comes to you for a cuddle, please do! If you like to watch television with him on your lap, please do! If you want him to sleep in your bedroom, please do! But if you are having problems, these are the areas that you may have to change.

It is important not to apply these suggestions on a blanket basis but pay more attention to exactly what motivates your dog. These are simply areas that may need to be brought under your control in order to create a relationship based on effective communication and friendly co-operation.

TRAINING USING MODERN POSITIVE TECHNIQUES

Given the right attitude and correct equipment and a good degree of patience, it is relatively easy for you to train your Boxer to respond happily to the usual everyday commands. Even though sometimes he may be easily distracted and all too playful when you expect him to concentrate, training him to 'sit', 'stay', 'come', 'lie down', 'stay', 'come' and, most importantly, 'stop', is a simple question of persisting in trying to associate each of the signals from you with the desired response and then reinforcing the conditioned response by rewarding the behaviour.

Training methods

However, the traditional methods of achieving these simple, enjoyable aims actually militate against the teaching process and cannot be justified now that we understand much more about how dogs learn. The use of loud voices, choke chains ('check chains') and physical punishment are increasingly a thing of the past, and modern educated trainers and behaviourists believe that these are no longer acceptable for training dogs. Threatening training techniques using such punishing methods can cause more physical and psychological harm than good;

kinder methods based on motivational techniques are far more effective.

A well-trained dog is a pleasure to own but, to be effective, training should be enjoyable for both dog and owner.

When to start training

It is essential to disregard another piece of traditional nonsense in the world of dogs: the debarring of dogs from some training classes until they are at least six months old. This is the very time when they are becoming more competitive and entering the difficult and distracting phase of adolescence. As with children, the earlier your Boxer starts learning the

PUPPY CLASSES AND PARTIES

When run by assessed and approved trainers, these are designed to help you train your puppy and will take pups up to the age of about eighteen weeks – just before the onset of sexual maturity when their behaviour also starts to be motivated by new hormonal influences. Puppy parties for dogs up to the age of about ten weeks, and classes for ten- to eighteen-week-olds are often held at veterinary surgeries and usefully incorporate discussions and assistance on vaccinations, worming and other aspects of general healthcare.

better and, while the concentration span of a six- to eight-week-old puppy, or even a six- to eight-month-old juvenile dog, may be quite low, the sooner you start training him with positive techniques and the right equipment, the better.

Reward and non-reward

Our job in training dogs is to motivate them through the prospect of gaining

It is not difficult to train a Boxer if you start early and use kind, reward-based training methods as in this book.

rewards to behave as we wish them to by signalling our behaviour and intents effectively and clearly. Then a dog can not only interpret our requirements but can also take comfort from a consistent, positive and happy relationship.

EFFECTIVE COMMUNICATION

One of the major common features of behaviour problems in dogs is that effective communication between the owner and his dog has either failed to develop properly or has become confusing for the dog. The owner's voice and the dog's name have usually come to mean different things at different times and one of the first jobs of treatment is to introduce some forms of communication that are consistent and readily comprehensible to the dog. Signalling rewards in Pavlovian style is easy enough, and every dog learns very quickly that a smiling face, high voice and rattle of the biscuit tin is associated with a rewarding experience. However, a basic error that owners often make is to assume that 'punishment' is the opposite of 'reward' and that threatening or smacking a dog will decrease the frequency or expression of their pet's unwanted behaviour.

Not so. The opposite of reward is 'non-reward', not punishment, and letting your dog know this through a signal is just as easy as signalling rewards for behaviour that you do wish to encourage and teach your dog.

Reinforcement and reward

■ **A reinforcement,** either positive or negative, is often something that happens when an act is occurring and is therefore seen to be received as a direct consequence of something that the dog is doing. So a positive reinforcement is anything that occurs during a particular act that the dog finds pleasant and therefore is likely to increase the possibility that the behaviour will be repeated. For example, a dog finds dropped scraps at the base of a child's high chair and quickly learns to take up a 'ready-to-forage' position as soon as the child is placed in it at mealtimes.

■ **A reward** is something that is positive and pleasurable to the dog and which usually happens after an act has occurred: a form of payment for a job well done. The difference between a reward and a reinforcement is often in its timing.

A reward must be offered immediately after the behaviour that earned it in order for it to be associated with that behaviour. Any delay in rewarding a specific action could result in subsequent unwanted behaviour being rewarded instead. For example, if there is sufficient delay between a dog sitting when asked and the giving of the titbit reward to the point where he receives the titbit after standing up again, he may be trained to 'sit and stand up' on the command 'sit'.

Types of reward

There are three distinct types of reward.

■ **Intentional reward**

Using intentional rewards does not require many hours of drill-type training, choke chains or harsh voices. It's simply a matter of letting your dog find out what he needs to do to earn the reward.

■ For example, you can teach your dog to sit on command just by holding and showing him a titbit above his head, just out of reach, and then moving it slightly behind his head. Ignore any efforts to snatch at the titbit and close your hand if he makes a grab. Frustrated at not being able to obtain the titbit, he will usually try alternative behaviours and will sit down to get a better look at the food.

■ The instant his bottom hits the floor, say 'sit' to associate the word with the position and give him his reward. Next time he is presented with the titbit in similar circumstances, he will remember that he had to sit down in order to obtain it and after a couple of similarly rewarding experiences will often sit without being asked when he sees the titbit. He will have taught himself how to earn the reward; our job will have been simply to associate the word 'sit' with the behaviour so that we may use it more broadly and without always having to proffer a titbit.

■ **Unintentional reward**
We can often encourage problems for ourselves by giving inadvertent or unintentional rewards to dogs. A good example of this can be seen in attention-demanding dogs. If a dog picks up one of

his toys while we are on the phone, we ignore it. If he picks up one of our shoes, we interrupt the telephone conversation to tell him off and take the shoe away. As attention of any sort, be it scolding or praising, is seen as success, he repeats the behaviour next time the phone rings and one begins to wonder who is training whom. Such dogs are not intrinsically disobedient or problem dogs; in fact, they are usually very clever and certainly very good at training our behaviour. Being 'disobedient' can easily become a learned trait through rewarding behaviour that we didn't intend to and often without realizing that we were rewarding the dog.

■ Survival reward

The outcome of some behaviours rewards a dog much more than anything we can offer. Dogs have one purpose in life and that is to remain fit and healthy in order to survive. To do this in challenges or conflicts they use one of the four 'F' strategies (see page 29). For example, if a dog has not been socialized properly towards people when young, he may be fearful of strangers as an adult and his coping 'strategy' may be to threaten to 'fight' or actually to attack strangers. This policy usually results in the stranger backing off which, for the dog, functions as the reward. He thinks that he has 'saved his own life', an ultimate form of reward which quickly reinforces the use of aggression in similar circumstances in the future.

■ Trying to distract the dog with a titbit in such circumstances will not over-ride this ultimate reward because he is trying physically to survive at the time, and will not be interested in eating to survive for later. In these cases, we need to precondition an avoidance response (see below) and switch the dog's attention back to the owner and then apply reinforcement training techniques to teach him to adopt a different behaviour in the same or similar circumstances in future.

FRUSTRATIVE NON-REWARD

The withdrawal or omission of an expected reward is known as 'non-reward' (see page 42). This causes frustration in dogs and other animals, and the greater the expected reward, the greater the frustration. However, when a sound or other signal is introduced as a signal of non-reward, this in itself does not induce frustration. The animal withdraws from the signal and this action actually becomes a reward because it reduces their frustration. This is known as 'passive avoidance' and, through it, dogs learn to refrain from behaviours that will lead to unrewarding consequences.

Dog Training Discs

These were developed by the canine behaviourist John Fisher to enable dog owners to signal 'non-reward' and therefore encourage calm resignation in a dog when confronted with something that previously made him over-excited or made him behave 'badly'.

Dog Training Discs are five brass discs on a fob which, when shaken, make a rather unique sound. However, it is not the sound itself but the introductory process of the discs that makes them so effective in training dogs and treating problem behaviour.

■ The introduction involves presenting the dog with an expected reward and then calmly removing it as he approaches it.

This is usually performed by dropping a few favoured titbits on the floor. The dog will move to take the titbits, intentions and behaviours that he sees as rewarding.

■ The owner or trainer then drops the Discs near the dog and removes the titbits as he stoops to eat them. After four or five repetitions, or perhaps a few more with easily distracted Boxers, the dog learns that the sound of the discs is a signal of 'frustrative non-reward' or failure of his intents to take and eat the titbits.

■ He may look confused and frustrated at his failure to gain the titbits and usually turns to his owner for some reassurance. This should be offered immediately, as comfort from the owner is a safety signal that relieves the dog's frustration at having failed in his previous intentions.

■ This introduction procedure teaches the dog a passive avoidance response; in future, he will not attempt to move towards the titbits whenever he hears the sound. But this is only the introduction procedure; the sound of the Dog training Discs can now be used to help

interrupt any unwanted actions.

■ When the dog hears the sound, he avoids completing the behaviour he was intent on and returns quietly to his owner. Because he is automatically in a relaxed state, he can be encouraged to perform a different behaviour.

■ Dogs do not get used to the sound or learn to ignore the Discs provided they are introduced properly and away from any particular problem behaviour to establish them as a clear signal of non-reward. Because the sound is consistent in tone, it can be used effectively by any member of the family. Once the dog is conditioned to respond to the Discs, he will react in a similar prompt way to how he reacts to a signal of reward, e.g. rattling the biscuit tin, irrespective of which member of the family rattles it.

THE GENTLE LEADER SYSTEM

This was developed in the United States by top veterinarian Professor Bob Anderson and Ruth Foster, a former President of the National Association of Obedience Instructors. The Gentle Leader is a comfortable nylon headcollar which is designed specifically for dogs, and adapts to fit the contours of each individual dog's face. Its action depends upon being fitted to the dog's head in order to be able to control the whole dog, as where the head goes, the body must follow. Unfortunately, if your Boxer has a very flat face, there may be an insufficient length of muzzle or 'stop' on which to fit the noseloop of the Gentle Leader and so it will not be suitable. In this instance, turn to page 52 for an alternative but equally kind approach to training him.

How the Gentle Leader works

This scientific concept has been designed to help owners mimic the way that dogs naturally communicate and has a unique mode of action that takes account of canine behaviour. Dogs have a natural instinct to pull against pressure, whether

on choke or regular collars, and will do so even though pressure on the throat causes pain and choking and their owners may yank, tug and shout to try and stop them pulling.

The Gentle Leader does not choke a dog. It is designed scientifically to direct the dog's entire body by controlling his head and nose, but it also dissuades him from pulling on the lead by transferring some of his forward energy to the back of his neck via the neckstrap when he tries to pull forwards. Puppies instinctively relax when their mother picks them up and pressure is applied to the scruff of their necks. This is a natural adaptation for survival as it enables her to transport them with minimal fuss to escape from enemies.

■ Dogs of any age often respond instinctively with relaxed subordination when their pack leader gently grasps their muzzle with his mouth. This demonstrates the pack leader's authority, but in a calm and reassuring manner, not an aggressive one. The Gentle Leader's noseloop encircles your dog's nose and jaw and acts in the same manner as a pack-leader's mouth, communicating your natural leadership. Your dog's instinctive resistance to all these influences and redirected pressures cause him to stop pulling to relieve the pressure at the back of the head and to relax and walk easily by your side.

■ The Gentle Leader therefore gives owners natural effective leadership, kind control and 'power steering'. Thus it is recommended especially for controlling boisterous dogs, and for all dogs that pull on the lead, and enables owners to train their dog at home and outdoors to be sociable and obedient, calmly, quickly and effectively. This even saves the time, effort and expense of taking a dog to training classes, although many instructors use the Gentle Leader as a standard item of equipment to enable them to train with positive techniques.

Get started

At home or in training classes, all you will need aside from the Gentle Leader is your dog's usual lead, a supply of his favourite small titbits or a favourite toy to use as rewards, along with a positive, happy and rewarding attitude and a little patience, especially with young dogs.

The ideal place to begin to train your puppy or older dog is where he is most relaxed, at home and in the garden. Once he has learned the signals of reward and non-reward and grown accustomed to wearing his lead, collar and Gentle Leader, follow the simple procedures overleaf. When he has grasped the basics, take him to some new places and repeat the plan so that he comes to behave calmly and accept your instructions everywhere you are together.

BASIC TRAINING

1 Stopping pulling on the lead

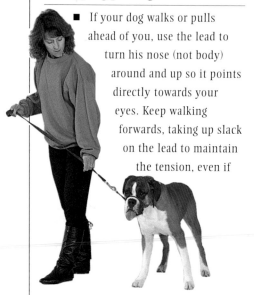

- If your dog walks or pulls ahead of you, use the lead to turn his nose (not body) around and up so it points directly towards your eyes. Keep walking forwards, taking up slack on the lead to maintain the tension, even if your dog pulls backwards or sits.
- When you reach his side, praise and encourage him to walk beside you. To keep him at your side and prevent him pulling ahead, anticipate his action and gently raise his nose as soon as his shoulder passes your leg. His instinctive response will cause him to halt momentarily to relieve the pressure on the back of his neck, causing him to slow down and stop pulling.
- Walk on immediately with more words of encouragement. Never jerk the lead or tell your dog off if he is a little slow to learn – this will frighten him and make him even slower. Simply repeat the above in gentle fashion until he understands how to walk calmly beside you without pulling.

2 Walking/jogging to heel

- Stand to one side of your dog and hold the lead in your hand, leaving a maximum of 5 cm (2 in) of slack where it joins the lead attachment ring under his chin. Fold any excess lead into your other hand.
- Talk to him in a friendly, encouraging voice and start walking forwards. If your dog holds back, keep walking, coaxing him with some kind words and perhaps the motivating sight of a favourite toy or titbit.
- At the same time, pull gently forwards on the lead and quickly release the tension as soon as he sets off. He will soon learn that good things happen when he comes to your side.
- Begin by asking him to 'walk' and set off walking at your normal pace, keeping him at your side. Then ask him to 'run' while steadily increasing your pace to a gentle trot, keeping him by your side and speaking to him encouragingly. Increase slowly to your normal jogging pace, encouraging him to 'jog' as you go.

3 'Sit'

- Hold the lead in your right hand. Pull it forwards and upwards to point your dog's nose gently skywards. As you tip his nose up, his head should go gently back and his hindquarters will lower to the ground.
- As soon as they touch the ground, say 'sit' in an encouraging voice, release the tension on the lead and allow his head to move freely, and offer him a titbit.
- He may stand up again immediately, especially if he is young, but repeat several times and he will soon associate the sitting position with the word 'sit' and will respond without needing to lift his head.

4 'Stay'

- Hold the lead in your left hand with 5 cm (2 in) of slack, and hold a reward of a titbit in your right hand.
- Give the command 'stay' from directly in front of the dog, raising the palm of your right hand to face him, while still holding the titbit. If he tries to move forwards or take the reward, pull up gently on the lead with your left hand, at the same

BASIC TRAINING

'Stay' continued

time moving towards the dog and repeating the command, 'stay'.

■ After a few seconds, move towards him and reward his patience by lowering your right hand to give him the titbit.

■ Gradually increase the 'stay' time until your dog has learned to 'stay' for a minute or so. You may wish to extend the distance between you, so walk slowly backwards with the palm of your right hand raised to face him while repeating the 'stay' command until you have reached the length of the lead. If he moves towards you, remind him to 'stay' by pulling gently up on the lead and then quickly releasing it. Then begin again from close by, repeating the command 'stay'.

■ To extend the distance beyond the length of the lead, retreat to its full extent, lay it on the ground and continue to retreat slowly with your palm raised, facing your dog as before, while you repeat the 'stay' command.

■ When he has remained in the 'stay' long enough, return to him calmly and reward and praise him; do not call him to you to be rewarded for the stay, or you will be rewarding the 'come'. Gradually increase the time he remains in the 'stay' and lengthen the distance.

5 'Down'

■ Teach 'down' while your dog is in the 'sit' position at your left side. Hold a toy or a food reward in your hand about 2.5 cm (1 in) in front of his nose.

■ With his nose following the reward, bring your hand slowly straight down to the floor and, while saying 'down', move the object slowly away from the dog at floor level to induce him to lie down.

■ Do not push down on his back or withers as he will push back up and resist going 'down'. Sometimes you can

6 'Come'

■ To maintain your leadership/control during training, attach your dog's lead to the Gentle Leader so that you can control the distance between you and your dog as you teach, to prevent him running away when you give the command 'come'. An extending lead is very useful to extend the range of training this response.

■ Begin with your dog sitting in front of you. Take a favourite toy or titbit and place it on the palm of your hand. Kneel on one knee to lower your profile, offer less potential threat to your dog and make yourself more attractive to approach.

■ Extend your forearm and your hand showing the attractive reward, giving the command 'come' with an enthusiastic

■ Repeat the command 'down' as soon as he adopts the correct position. After he has learned 'down', follow the instructions in the previous section for the 'stay' command to teach him to stay down when asked.

encourage him to obey the 'down' command by drawing the reward under a low table so that he must go down underneath it in order to get to the reward.

between you to a pace or two and then steadily further away, repeating the whole process at each increase. Do not proceed too fast or too far, or the dog may fail to obey and get distracted. If that happens, gently pull on the lead to turn his head towards you, but quickly release the tension as soon as you have his attention.

gentle voice. As the dog steps towards you, say 'good dog' as praise and show your hand, palm up, for him to take the reward without enthusiastic nipping of your fingers to get at it!

■ Your dog will only have to take a step forward to gain his reward initially, but as soon as he learns to come when called, extend the distance

HANDS-OFF TRAINING

Training with the Gentle Leader is based on initially having good physical control of your dog, but not all dogs need this. Training classes are perfect for some, but not for others. If you would like to train your dog between putting the kettle on and making a cup of tea, or want to practise what you already know during the commercial breaks, the 'Hands-off'

technique which was refined by one of the co-authors of this book, Sarah Whitehead, is probably ideal. It is great fun with puppies and keen-to-please adult dogs, such as Boxers. In an ideal world, all dogs would wait for a human hand to come towards them with excitement and longing, knowing that it means affection, enjoyable physical contact and the prospect of food. 'Hands-off' training means teaching just that.

Coming when called

- Standing in front of your dog, call him in a friendly voice: 'George come!'
- Waggle the food lure in your outstretched hand and start moving backwards. If your dog shows no response, run, scream, flap your arms etc. until he looks at you.

- Then, with the food on your dog's nose, move backwards, just one or two paces. If the dog moves just one step towards you, he's yours, so give him the reward.
- Gradually increase the distance he has to come to get the food, then graduate to the point where someone else holds him for you while you walk away, calling him and offering a juicy titbit. As soon as he reaches you, touch his collar and give him the treat.

'Sit'

■ Show your dog a food treat in your right hand, concentrating on keeping the food in view and close to his nose.

■ Lift your hand up and back so he has to look right up to follow your fingers. The movement of looking upwards causes his rear end to go down and suddenly your dog is sitting!

■ As soon as his backside hits the ground, give him the food reward, or you may reward the wrong behaviour, e.g. wriggling, barking or scratching.

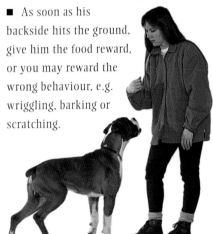

■ Do this a few times to check the positioning of your hand is correct. Now you can say the word 'sit' just before you move the food lure. In a matter of minutes you have taught your dog a verbal request to sit, plus a really effective hand signal. All you need to do now is practise until he's really quick to respond and totally reliable.

■ From now on, simply ask your dog to sit before he gets anything in life that he likes: e.g. his dinner, his lead.

'Down'

■ With the food lure close to your dog's nose, lower your hand right down to the floor directly between his front paws. Hold on to the treat by turning your palm down with the food hidden inside your hand. This way the dog will want to burrow his nose underneath and he will turn his head sideways to nibble the lure.

■ Early indications of imminent success are: your dog raising a paw to try and get the treat from your hand, and his front end going down in a play-bow position and moving backwards slightly. All these things mean that you just have to sit and wait!

■ Eventually his back end will flop down to the floor too and, at this

HANDS-OFF TRAINING

'Down' continued

instant, drop the treat on to the floor and allow him to eat it. (Dropping it prevents your dog from following your hand back up again like a yo-yo.)

■ Practice makes perfect! You can now add the word 'down' just before moving the food lure. For a dog who doesn't catch on too quickly, pass the food or toy under a low-level chair or table so that he drops down to follow the lure underneath it. Alternatively, you can arch your own leg for your dog to drop down under your knee.

Walking by your side

Dogs only pull on leads because we fit them to them and so it's usually easier to train a dog not to pull ahead by starting without one! When you ask a dog to walk to heel, you are really asking him to follow you, and the prospect of a tasty food treat will help motivate him to do just that.

■ Position your dog by your side by luring him with a food treat. (Hold the treat in your right hand if you want him to walk on the left-hand side and vice versa.)

■ Start by taking only two or three steps ahead and then immediately ask him to sit by your side by bringing your right hand across in front of him and luring him into the sit position with the treat. Keep eye contact all the time and try to maintain his concentration by showing him the food lure.

■ Once you begin to set off at a quicker pace, you will need to work hard to keep him in the right position. He may lag behind (so run forwards), he will move

ahead (so stop or walk backwards) or he may veer off to one side (so move in the opposite direction straightaway). Keep your dog guessing about your next move and he will stay close by, giving you the chance to reward him.

■ Start by encouraging him to follow you around the furniture in the house and keep your training sessions short and fun. Finally, you can attach the lead to his ordinary collar, but remember to keep it slack. Pretend that it's a piece of cotton which will break under even the slightest tension, and that way your dog will never have anything to pull against.

'Stay'

■ With the dog in the sit or down position, ask him to 'stay' and hold the food treat just above his nose. Count one second, give him the treat, then give him your release word 'OK'.

■ Next time, count two seconds, then give him the treat, release him, then count three seconds and repeat and so on.

■ Holding the food above can later be turned into a flat hand signal which indicates 'stop'.

■ Praise your dog all the time for being in the stay, but, apart from giving the release word at the end, don't say anything during training. This is because you want to praise and positively reinforce him for staying, not for getting up when the session is over.

■ Once your dog will stay for more than a minute, start to 'proof' the request by asking him to stay, and then take one step away.

PART TWO

CARING FOR YOUR DOG

Buying any puppy or acquiring an adult dog is a huge responsibility, and caring for any dog will take up a lot of your time over the next ten or so years. Therefore it is not a decision to be taken lightly but one that requires careful consideration by all the members of your family. Small Boxer puppies can look especially appealing but they should never be bought on impulse. Many people forget that these cute little creatures grow up into large powerful dogs. Boxers make good companions and loving family pets but, as with all large breeds, they need a great deal of exercise and lots of your attention. In this section on caring for your dog, you will find expert advice on choosing a puppy and looking after him; feeding, exercising and grooming your adult dog; and also how you can both enjoy the experience of showing your dog.

THE BOXER PUPPY

ACQUIRING A PUPPY

There is a saying in the dog world that most Boxer owners can take a joke. This is only half in jest, for a healthy sense of humour is an absolute essential for anyone who is considering owning this larger-than-life breed. Buying any puppy is a life-long commitment, and caring for any dog takes huge amounts of time, energy and money – all precious resources that very few of us have in abundance. However, buying a Boxer puppy requires perhaps even more careful consideration than buying a dog of any other breed, because although their size will develop to adult proportions, in their minds they never grow up. This is the real Peter Pan of the dog world. Boxers love life, and they just have to share their enthusiasm – whatever the circumstances, whatever you happen to be doing at the time!

Like many other large breeds, Boxers consume vast amounts of food, need a great deal of exercise once adult and an above-average commitment from their owners to socializing and training. They are an adaptable breed, and in the right environment they blossom into excellent companions, but do you really have the space, financial commitment and time for this kind of dog? Boxers are powerful, fast and full of energy when running around in the great outdoors. However, they still need to expend this energy if they are cooped up in a small environment, and therefore they are not ideally suited to life in a flat.

Consider your lifestyle

Take some time to think about your life-style. All puppies and dogs need company. They are social animals and their ancestral heritage means that most of them find it difficult to be isolated from the rest of their 'pack'. Wolves are rarely alone from the moment of birth to the moment of death, and leaving any dog at home alone requires training and understanding to enable the dog to learn to cope. Boxers are particularly prone to the effects of separation anxiety – they live for contact and attention from their human family, and as such are likely to

Cropped ears are still permissible in some European countries but thankfully this practice is outlawed in the UK.

BOXERS AND CHILDREN

Boxers are well known for their affection and gentleness with children. However, it should not be underestimated that they are large and powerful. Jumping up at people may be a friendly gesture, but is not appropriate when directed towards young children or infirm or elderly people. Children should not be left unsupervised with any dog, and certainly should not be allowed to tease them or play rough games which might end in tears.

be destructive when left alone at home for extended periods of time. If your family is out all day, think again about getting any kind of dog, let alone a Boxer, unless you are happy to rebuild your home once your Boxer has demolished it!

Finding the right breeder

If you have decided that a Boxer is the pet for you and you have the time, energy, money and commitment, your next step is to go about finding one that will suit your needs. Here are some helpful suggestions that you might like to consider.

Do your homework

If you are unsure of whether a Boxer is the right choice for you, or indeed if any dog will fit into your life at the present time, do some homework to discover what they are really like to live with. Borrow an adult Boxer for a weekend or find a well-established puppy class in your area, and go along to 'test-drive' a dog. Many people report that they did not know just how bouncy their Boxer puppy was going to be, and that if only they had had the opportunity to experience the real thing in action, they might have chosen differently.

Colour-match

Generally, Boxers are either fawn, red or brindle in colour. However, it is not unheard of for pure white Boxers to sometimes appear. These dogs are generally regarded as 'undesirable' by the show world, not least because hereditary deafness is sometimes associated with the colour. However, white Boxers are certainly eye catching and, like any other dog, make excellent pets when socialized and trained from an early age.

Be strong-minded

Finding a breeder who has puppies for sale is always best done through a responsible outlet. The Kennel Club (KC) holds lists of breeders who register their puppies, but a KC registration is no guarantee of either the quality or health of that puppy. Some organisations, e.g. PRO-Dogs in Great Britain, now have lists of breeders who agree to abide by an ethical code of practice, i.e. that they

have tested their stock for hereditary diseases and have raised their puppies in ideal conditions (for more details turn to page 144). Also, in the UK, a magazine (*Dogs Today*) promotes breeders who rear puppies indoors, have good results in all hereditary disease tests and provide a good after-sales service.

- Don't be tempted to buy a puppy from an advertisement in a newspaper, particularly where more than one breed is included for sale, or from a pet shop. Many are outlets for puppy farms where unscrupulous people breed puppies en masse in appalling conditions and without the necessary care over the health or temperament of their breeding stock or

with any thought to their socialization.

■ Always insist on seeing the mother and, even better, the father too when choosing a puppy. The mother's temperament and behaviour have an enormous influence on the puppies. Of course, the father gives fifty per cent of his genes and characteristics too, but very often a breeder may take a bitch to be mated to a stud dog that lives some distance away, and is therefore not around to be seen by you.

■ Never buy a puppy spontaneously, and never be tempted to buy one from anyone who offers to deliver the puppy to you, or to meet you half-way and exchange the puppy at a service station. Puppies are not like fast food – delivered to your home or ordered by credit card over the phone. The dog you choose will be with you for better or worse for well over the next decade – a lot of time to repent at leisure.

HEREDITARY DISEASES

■ Always ask the breeder about the health of their stock. Boxers can suffer from several different hereditary problems, including cleft palate, spinal, heart and skin problems and PA (a degeneration of the nervous system).

■ If choosing a white Boxer, it is important to be aware of the possibility that the puppy might be deaf. This does not necessarily preclude that dog from making a good pet, but prospective owners need to be aware of the extra effort and time they will need to invest in their dog's training and care.

Home comforts

■ Although it may be heart-breaking, never, ever, be tempted to buy a puppy that has not been born in the home of the person selling it. Puppies that have been born outside the home environment – even some of those born in immaculate kennels at the bottom of the breeder's garden – cannot have experienced enough of everyday life and contact with people, children and domestic environmental stimuli, e.g. the vacuum cleaner or the TV, and are unlikely to cope with them in later life. Steel yourself, and just walk away from any puppies that have not been born and raised in the home, or if the mother is not available for you to see, or if her temperament is unsound.

■ A mother of good temperament will be happy to see visitors and children, and will be confident enough in her environment and owners to allow you to handle, play with and pick up her puppies. Any mother that backs away, growls, snarls or appears in any way nervous, aggressive or subdued may have passed on these traits to her puppies. Do not take the risk – you will be the one to pay for it later.

■ Be prepared for the breeder to ask you lots of questions about your lifestyle and the commitment you can give to your puppy. Some may even want to see photographs of your garden. This shows a caring and responsible attitude towards the future of their puppy. Be suspicious if the only question asked is how you would like to pay.

■ With this in mind, it may be that you have to wait for the right puppy from the right breeder to be born. Don't forget that joy from your dog for the next twelve or so years is worth waiting for now.

■ It is also worth remembering that the more a puppy experiences before you even bring him home, the more confident, outgoing and steady he is likely to be as a juvenile and as an adult. With this in mind, one-off pet dog breeders can sometimes be your best option as long as they are not attempting to breed for profit (if done properly, breeding puppies is never profitable) and the bitch is a confident, friendly much-loved family pet.

Socialization

Puppies go through various stages of development, and the most crucial of these is the socialization period, from three to twelve weeks old. This is the time during which much of your puppy's adult behaviour and character will be determined. Considering that more than

Puppies need human contact from the earliest possible age.

half of this time is likely to be spent with the breeder, it is absolutely critical that this is not wasted, or indeed ruined by bad experiences.

Choose an average pup

Probably the most important factor to look for when choosing a puppy as a pet is to choose the most average. Many people report that their puppy chose them, by running up, pushing all the other puppies out of the way, and demanding their attention. This may well be the puppy to choose if you are an experienced owner with a very strong personality and boundless energy, but in the wrong hands this dog may well end up ruling the roost within two months of settling in at home.

■ Equally unsuitable is the puppy that does not want to approach you, and sits at the back of the litter, or hides behind his mother or litter-mates. Some dogs like this may turn out to be highly intelligent and quick to learn – they usually have to use brain rather than brawn to win food and contests with their litter-mates. However, the risks of problems of nervousness or anxiety are likely to be increased. The puppy that is happy to see you, happy to be picked up, handled and played with, is not overly daunted by a sudden sound such as a hand-clap and plays well with his litter-mates is likely to be the most well-balanced, all-round ideal pet dog.

One dog or two?

■ When you see the litter for the first time, be sensible and try not to be overcome by the cuteness of the puppies in front of you. If you are in any doubt, leave them there. A good breeder should be happy for you to go away and think about it, and come back to see the puppies again if necessary, rather than rushing you into making a decision.

■ Also, do not be tempted to take two puppies at the same time, even if your heart is breaking at the thought of leaving one puppy behind on his own. Two puppies of the same age, particularly litter-mates, are a recipe for disaster. It is vital to understand that

WHICH ONE FOR YOU?

Choosing a puppy to be an ideal pet from a litter is not an easy task. Obviously, if you have a preference for choosing a dog or a bitch this will narrow your choice. Generally speaking, females are easier to train and can be less competitive in a family environment than males. It is possible that females are more likely to be good natured with other dogs. Males can sometimes be overly-macho, squaring up to other males and making early interactions with other dogs very important. However, both will require the same amount of veterinary treatment, socialization, exercise, training and general care.

although dogs settle well and live in harmony with a human social group, we are a different species. One dog in a human social group learns to interact and communicate with us to be able to survive, and this is where the man/dog bond is formed. Put two dogs together into such an environment and they will interact with each other, often to the exclusion of humans, and sometimes to the exclusion of other types of dog, too.

■ If you have already decided that you would like two dogs, be patient and wait until you have formed a relationship, socialized and trained one dog through to adolescence – all of which takes a

LEAVING THE LITTER

The time when most breeders allow puppies to leave their mother and go to a new home varies enormously. Puppies need to stay in their own litter and with their mother to learn about dog language – how dogs interact with each other socially – and to be taught vital information by their mother. During the first few weeks of life, puppies play a great deal with each other in the litter – practising how it feels to win contests for food, toys or attention and experimenting with body language which they will later come to recognise as signals of intent connected with dominance, submission, appeasement, pacification, possession and rejection.

surprising length of time, and then think about getting another. Two puppies together are rarely double the joy – only double the trouble.

Weaning

This is a vital time when puppies learn to cope with frustration by experiencing rejection from the mother when they want to feed (for more about this, refer to Chapter 8), and this is another very good reason why you should insist that puppies are raised with the bitch. However, during this time, it is also vital that puppies are learning about people: that some of our body language is different to theirs, and that we are friendly and non-threatening.

- Socialization with people must therefore start early in the breeder's home. No puppy should be removed from his litter before he is six weeks old and, generally, no later than eight weeks. However, the fact that most puppies will not be able to have contact with other puppies of the same age for at least the next four weeks, because their vaccination programmes may not be complete, may mean that it is better for them to be left in the canine educational sector – the litter – until eight weeks, so that they can learn the rules and signals of canine communication.

- Dogs that have not had sufficient contact with humans prior to eight weeks are likely to be prone to developing behavioural problems connected with people, whereas those given lots of human contact, but taken too early from the litter, are likely to have missed out on canine company and may display aggression to other dogs later on – a problem that is extremely difficult to cure if severe.

Planning for the puppy's arrival

Bringing your puppy home is an exciting event, particularly if you have had to wait for some time for the right puppy. A little planning before the excitement sets in is a good idea, particularly if you have a long journey ahead of you, another dog at

Be gentle with your new puppy as he settles into your home.

home to whom you are going to introduce your new puppy, a cat, or another pet.

■ Ideally, take a piece of cloth or an old towel with you to the breeder's home when you visit your puppy to make final arrangements. Ask the breeder to put this under the mother's blankets, or in her bed, so that it will be covered with her scent when you bring it home with the pup. You can also do a 'scent exchange', by making sure the cloth or towel already has some of your scent on it (putting it in the laundry bin or under your sheets usually has this effect) so that your puppy will already be familiar with your scent before he comes home with you.

The journey home

Try to prepare your car for the journey home – particularly if it is a long one. A large cardboard box or a bundle of towels are a good idea. You will need someone to help out by looking after the puppy in the back of the car for you if you are driving, and, as puppies usually have a habit of being sick on long car journeys, towels and clean-up tissues are a useful measure.

Be prepared

Make sure that you have as much information as possible from the breeder before you pick up your puppy. You will need to have bought the puppy some of the food that he is already used to eating, booked him in for his vaccination jabs, found a local puppy socialization class, checked out when you next need to give worming tablets, planned where he is going to sleep, and have a lightweight collar and lead ready and waiting.

Beds for puppies

Most puppies chew absolutely everything, so it is probably not worth investing huge amounts on an expensive bed. Puppies prefer the security of a small cosy nest rather than a vast expanse of bed to begin with, so a large cardboard box, lined with a cosy blanket, is ideal. Wrapping a towel, which has been impregnated with the mother's and litter-mates' familiar smells, around a warm hot water bottle provides snug security.

Meeting other animals

Most young puppies are quite cautious about meeting new creatures, such as an older dog or a cat, but some forethought will help this to go smoothly.

■ Firstly, it is up to all the humans in the family to constantly remind their established older dog that he still has pride of place and is boss of all he surveys. Making the mistake of telling the older dog off for trying to sniff the puppy or, later, for reprimanding it, can seriously damage the two dogs' future relationship.

■ If your established dog is generally good with other dogs and puppies, it is ideal to allow him to meet the puppy off home territory – in the front garden if necessary – and allow him as much free rein as possible to investigate and get to know the newcomer.

■ Try to ignore the puppy, but praise and talk to your older dog all the time he is showing gentle interest. Allow your older dog to walk into the house first, and then follow with the puppy.

■ It is essential that you establish recognition of the puppy as a subordinate to your older dog straight away. Roles may be reversed later on, but initially the puppy must not be put in a position where he appears to be competing for your attention as a resource.

■ Food is a valuable resource to a dog and an older dog may defend it if the puppy comes too close, so exercise some caution at meal times.

■ At other times, it is usually best not to interfere if your older dog disciplines the puppy, as long as he is not actually damaging him. As the days and weeks go by most puppies take enormous liberties with their older dog companions such as hanging off their ears and biting their legs in play. In this situation, it is essential that your older dog does sometimes use a little inhibited discipline to teach the puppy that he cannot behave in this way.

■ If you are worried about your older dog's reaction to a newcomer in his house, use the protection of the puppy's play pen or crate to introduce the dogs – a safety cage is essential where the response of the other dog is an unknown quantity.

■ If you are aware that your older dog is not usually friendly with other dogs, seek advice from a behaviour counsellor regarding your existing dog's behaviour before making the decision to get another.

■ As the owner of two dogs, it is vitally important that you set aside a good deal of time to give to your new puppy individually. Most puppies bond extremely quickly to a tolerant older dog, and while it is rewarding to watch them play together and their relationship develop, it should not be to the exclusion of yours. It is vital that you build an equally individual relationship with the second dog as with the first. This means devoting time and energy to your puppy, away from his new canine friend.

Cats and puppies

Introducing a puppy to a cat in the household is also an important part of making sure that harmony reigns. Boxers are usually very friendly and inquisitive with other animals, but the vital element for a successful introduction is to allow your cat a clear escape route or vantage point to jump up on, without allowing your puppy to experience the thrill of the chase. Generally, a cat that is confident around dogs will quickly establish itself as boss, but introductions should always be done with the puppy restrained, by being held on a lead, with the cat free to escape if necessary. Obviously, you must put the cat's food and water up out of the puppy's reach, and also prevent the puppy from ambushing the cat while he is vulnerable on the litter tray.

SETTLING INTO THE NEW HOME

Puppies vary greatly in their response to being taken away from their mother and litter-mates and brought into a completely new environment. Some are as bold as brass and walk in as if they are already at home. Others are more shy and require some gentle, quiet time, giving them the opportunity to explore at their own pace. Try to discourage children from overwhelming the puppy at this important stage.

Play pens and crates

If there is one piece of equipment that is likely to save your sanity over the first few weeks of puppy ownership, it is an indoor kennel – sometimes called a crate – or, even better, a mesh play pen. Young puppies need huge amounts of sleep, and although they may appear to be constantly on the go, they suddenly flop down and take a nap. This,

and the fact that we cannot supervise them constantly, makes a play pen or crate an absolute essential in terms of allowing us to relax, without worrying that if the puppy is quiet he must be up to something naughty.

■ Far from being a cage to incarcerate your puppy when he has done wrong, a play pen or crate, if introduced gradually and with pleasant associations such as food and toys, is regarded by the dog as his cosy den – a secure area where he knows he will not be disturbed. Crates are also ideal for later use in the car, or away from home, e.g. when staying with friends overnight.

House-training

Using a crate also facilitates speedy house-training. This can be quick and painless for all concerned, and need never involve any form of punishment.

■ Of course, young puppies cannot be expected to have total control over their bodily functions, and the occasional accident is to be expected. However, by using an approach called 'errorless learning', puppies quickly learn what is expected of them and do their utmost to relieve themselves in the right place.

■ Errorless learning means never allowing your puppy to make a mistake by urinating or defecating in the wrong place. You can learn to predict when your puppy will need to go to the toilet – usually this is after playing, after waking up, after any kind of excitement, such as the children coming home from school, and straight after meals.

■ At these times, take your puppy to the same place outside and wait with him, even in the rain. Gently repeating a word or phrase, such as 'Be quick,' helps your puppy to remember why he's there.

As soon as your puppy starts to sniff around, or circle, praise him very gently, but genuinely. When he has been to the toilet, you can lavish him with praise and give him a really special titbit to reward him for his brilliance.

■ In between these events it is wise to take your puppy outside about once an hour, just in case he should need to go, and also to watch him closely for tell-tale signs, such as sniffing or circling.

■ If you wait outside with your puppy and nothing happens, bring him back inside. At this point you know that he has not been and is likely to need to go in the next little while. It is then up to you to supervise him constantly, so that you can watch him all the time. If you cannot do so, then either you need to put him in the crate or play pen, or in an enclosed area where you do not mind if he has an accident. The advantage of confining your puppy for very short periods when you cannot supervise him is that most dogs do not want to soil their sleeping area, and will therefore try to wait until you take them out again.

■ If you catch your puppy in the act of going, or about to go, at any other time, say 'Outside' in an urgent voice, and then take him quickly outside to show him where you do want him to go – even if it's too late to save your carpet. If you get even one drop in the right

place you can then praise your puppy.

■ Being cross with your puppy for making a mistake in the house is pointless. Dogs soon learn to associate any mess with your anger – not with the act of going – and simply show fear when you find it. The expression 'he knows what he has done; he even looks guilty' really means that the dog is showing fear when you are around. Dogs do not feel guilty for what they have done – they just learn to be scared of the consequences of your presence. It takes years for a child to be fully toilet-trained, but nobody would consider punishing a baby for having an accident in an inappropriate place. Old-fashioned punishments, e.g. rubbing the dog's nose in his mess, are abhorrent and

counter-productive and shouldn't be used.

■ Many people use sheets of newspaper to teach their puppy where to go to the toilet, but compared with the 'errorless' approach this is harder work in the long term as you need to house-train your puppy twice – first to newspaper and then outdoors.

■ Puppies that leak urine when meeting new people or dogs, or when greeting the family, are not showing a lack of house-training but are communicating their deference in a submissive way. They may roll over, sit with one hind leg held out to the side, or squirm along the floor when meeting someone or something they regard as being over-dominating. They may accompany this behaviour with urinating. Ignoring the puppy until you get outside, or crouching down and greeting him side-on, without looking at him directly, often helps, as it reassures the puppy that you are calm, gentle and friendly.

SLEEPLESS NIGHTS

During the first few nights that the puppy is away from his mother and litter-mates, it is likely that he will cry out if he feels lonely and isolated in the dark. Traditionally, pet owners were always told to ignore this crying and not to return to the dog at all costs, to prevent him establishing bad habits from day one. However, modern thought relies more on the dog's behaviour as a social animal and the fact that he is crying through distress and anxiety, and not being 'naughty'. Most puppies settle much better in their new home if they are not totally isolated from the family, and compromise is required. If you have a pen or crate for your puppy, allowing him to be in the bedroom with you for the first few nights is not a problem, as you can minimize any mess, give your puppy some reassurance simply by your physical proximity and judge when he needs to be taken out to relieve himself.

■ Try not to respond to every whimper if he is in the same room, as it is important that you do not teach him to cry for attention. It might be tempting to give in and allow your cuddly puppy to snuggle under the duvet with you, but this is probably not advisable – unless you will be happy to continue doing this once your pup has grown into a hulking 30-kg (66-lb) mass of muddy paws and slobber!

■ Once your puppy has overcome the novelty of his new surroundings, and is beginning to form a bond with the family, he should be confident enough to be moved downstairs to sleep, if you wish. Of course, this is more practical in many ways, as being able to control the bladder and bowels for the whole night is something that comes gradually, and most kitchen floors are easier to clean.

Food, glorious food

Boxers are infamous for their ability to eat anything and everything. These are dogs that are not just motivated by food; they live for it! Of course, this not only makes them easy to feed, but also easy to train. However, care must be taken that they do not put on too much weight. As puppies, extra weight can put pressure on the developing bones and muscles, whereas later on it puts extra strain on the dog's heart and hips.

Diet sheets

Most reputable breeders provide new pet owners with a diet sheet as a guide to the pup's requirements over the following weeks. However, much confusion arises over diet sheets, with owners not realising that more, less or different food

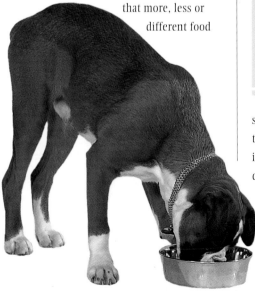

COLLARS AND LEADS

All dogs are required by law to wear a collar and identification disc when out and about. It is a good idea to get your puppy used to wearing a very soft, lightweight collar as soon as possible, and then to sometimes attach a very light lead to it in order that the strange feeling of something around the neck is gradually introduced. Some excellent nylon collars, which are now available, allow you to expand the collar as the puppy grows, meaning that you don't have to keep buying the next size up.

should be given as the dog grows, and that the sheet should be adapted to the individual dog's requirements. Diet sheets can sometimes be over-simplistic or, alternatively, bordering on the fanatical. If your dog's diet sheet looks like something from an *à la carte* restaurant menu and you find yourself drooling over it, then don't be afraid to try alternatives or ask your vet for advice.

PROTECT AND SOCIALIZE YOUR PUPPY

Because of the risks of the various diseases that can affect dogs, it is important that your puppy is inoculated. This inevitably means a delay in being able to take your puppy out to mix freely with other dogs, as he will need to have completed his vaccination programme before you can do so. However, the effects of under-socialization of puppies cannot be underestimated. It is thought that the greatest cause of euthanasia in dogs under two years of age is behavioural problems, so don't stop socializing your puppy for a second. If necessary, shop around for a vet who will provide the earliest possible vaccination programme for your puppy; the timing of the final injection still varies enormously, but your puppy should not be more than twelve weeks old at the stage where he can be taken out of your home safely.

Prior to this time, if you can't take the puppy to the outside world, then invite the outside world in to meet your puppy. Ask your friends, family and postman to visit. If you do not have children living at home, then invite some round.

Start young

Puppies love to learn. They are like little sponges absorbing information about

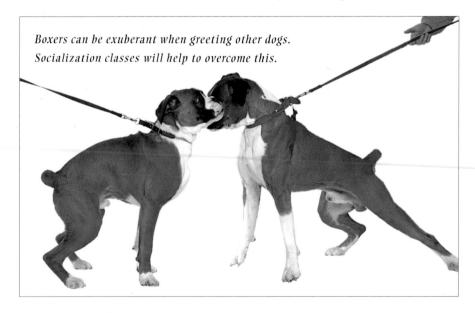

Boxers can be exuberant when greeting other dogs.
Socialization classes will help to overcome this.

their environment, the people around them, what feels good, and what does not. Traditionally, dogs had to wait until they were six months old before starting any kind of training. This was largely because old-fashioned training methods were too harsh for puppies any younger than this to cope with. However, with the advent of modern 'hands-off' methods of training, where the dog is motivated by food treats or toys and is not physically forced to comply, waiting until the puppy is six months old means that you have missed the easiest time in which to train and socialize him.

the kinds of snuffling noises they can make when playing together.

Socialization classes

Puppy socialization classes are now widely available and provide an excellent start for your puppy. Boxers particularly need significant amounts of contact with other people and other puppies of a similar age, not because they are unfriendly – quite the opposite. Most Boxers need to learn how to control their greeting behaviour so that they don't knock people or dogs over in their enthusiasm.

They also need a huge amount of contact with other puppies and dogs when young in order for them to learn how other dogs interact and the kind of body language they use. There is no doubt that other puppies sometimes do a 'double-take' at seeing a Boxer for the first time, and many are unsure about

Body language

It may be that the wrinkled face and markings of many adult Boxers make it particularly difficult for them to signal by facial expression alone that they are friendly and only want to play. Some less confident dogs may be open to misinterpreting a Boxer's bouncing approach as he comes hurtling across the park, making him a victim for defensive attacks by other dogs.

In order not to be left out of the play sessions, and to guard against being a victim of their unusual appearance later on, Boxers need to learn to adapt their body language to give clear messages of friendly intent, and a puppy class offers the perfect, safe opportunity for this lesson to occur.

Reward-based training

A good socialization class should have an upper age limit of around twenty weeks and should not simply be a free-for-all, with all the puppies constantly playing together. It is vital that the play is controlled, and that the basics of training, using reward-based methods only, are used. A good class should be able to show you how to build on the relationship you have with your puppy, and develop his willingness to your advantage.

Boxers are often 'good-natured thugs' at puppy classes. They have an enormous sense of humour and capacity for fun, but are also sensitive to their owner's moods, which makes light-hearted, reward-based training even more imperative. If put under stress or any kind of pressure, all dogs will choose to react by employing one of the four 'F' strategies, i.e. flight, fight, freeze or fiddle about (see page 29) – the Boxer's option is nearly always the latter.

This makes harsh or compulsive training entirely inappropriate. The Boxer fooling about in the corner of the hall in a more traditional class is not being 'naughty' but may be reacting to stress, and should not be there.

Handling your puppy

A good puppy class will also show you how to prevent many basic behavioural problems from ever occurring by being able to handle your puppy all over. This makes later veterinary examination, treatment and grooming easy and stress-free. Of course, at this age all puppies are wriggly, and it is important that they learn to associate being groomed and handled, having their feet touched and their mouths looked at with pleasant things. A tasty treat or an exciting toy is essential to distract your puppy while you practise, allowing you to accustom him to being inspected and touched all over. Start this procedure of friendly and enjoyable handling from day one and you will be training your dog to cope with later experiences, such as nail clipping and teeth cleaning, without a struggle.

Play biting

All puppies have needle-sharp teeth, and most of them appear to want to munch everything that moves. This is perfectly normal behaviour and is a vital stage of their development. Play biting allows the puppy to discover information about his environment, and also about just how hard he can bite other puppies, and humans. At this stage the puppy is learning a vital lesson called 'bite inhibition'.

■ Watching puppies play together makes sense of this. Most puppies play by biting each other; one will bite the other's leg while another will grab an ear and hold on. All this is entirely friendly and playful, unless one of the pups bites the other a little too hard. If this bite hurts the puppy, he will give a really impressive yelp and will refuse to play for the next few seconds. Once the pups have regained their composure, play resumes, but the bites will now be significantly more gentle.

■ This is an ideal way to teach our puppies that we too feel pain if they use our arms as pin cushions. Humans need

Accustom your dog to being handled from an early age.

to communicate that they are hurt when their puppies mouth them, not that they are angry, which puppies regard as irrational aggression. Ideally, we can yelp loudly or give a shout and then turn away as if to nurse our wounds. The puppy may look a little surprised when this first happens, but do not expect the biting to stop immediately. Gradually, over the next few weeks, the puppy biting should become increasingly gentle, until we yelp even at the slightest pressure. Finally, we can show pain if a puppy even puts his teeth on us; the rule is then that dogs can never bite humans, even in play – we are too fragile, and biting should cease altogether.

CHAPTER FOUR

THE ADULT DOG

DIET AND GENERAL CARE

All dogs are primed by their common development as hunter/scavengers through evolution over millions of years to take advantage of any food resource they can get their jaws on, but Boxers are experts. Feeding a Boxer is generally not difficult, if only because he will usually eat anything and everything – edible or not. However, there are a number of considerations that you should take into account when choosing an appropriate food for an adult Boxer.

Commercial pet foods

These are now the most common and popular choice for feeding the pet dog, being both convenient and relatively inexpensive. However, there are now a multitude of foods from which you can choose, and it is debatable as to whether the labelling of most of them provides adequate information for you to make an informed decision.

Finding a suitable diet

Boxers seem sensitive to diet in two respects: one is that they can sometimes put on weight easily, and an unsuitable diet could result in obesity which is difficult to shift and bad for your dog's health. The other is through their behaviour. Although this is difficult to prove statistically, anecdotal evidence implies that diet has many direct and indirect effects on dogs' behaviour and that an over-active dog, with little or no concentration span, may well be helped by a change in his diet.

■ All dogs, like people, are different and as such they have different requirements and varying reactions to specific ingredients or elements in their diet. It is therefore always useful to look at this aspect of a dog's care if a behavioural difficulty is experienced.

Types of dog food

Dog food is usually available as follows:
■ Moist food (in a can or chub)
■ Semi-moist, (usually packed in sealed plastic bags)
■ Dry food (often in flake or pellet form in a plastic-lined sack)

Adult Boxers are not generally fussy and will devour almost anything.

Whichever type of food you give to your Boxer, it is essential that you understand the manufacturer's feeding instructions which come with it.

Dog food is divided into two basic categories: complementary and complete. Most canned foods are described as complementary; this means that an additional biscuit or mixer is needed to add bulk to the diet and to balance its components. Conversely, many of the dried foods are complete, i.e. they do not require any additional food. In fact, adding anything to a dried food may disturb its balance.

A lot of behavioural and weight problems in dogs are caused by over-feeding, or feeding incorrectly. Adding a can of food to an already complete dried food is only asking for trouble.

Of course, it's not always possible to tell whether your dog is being adversely affected by the diet you are feeding. This is partly because it is often difficult to establish exactly what is in each food, and because if your dog looks well and healthy there may be no apparent reason to change what he eats.

Changing the diet

Studying your dog's health and behaviour may help you to decide whether his diet is suiting him. If your dog suffers regularly from one or more of the following conditions, it may indicate that

Healthy, well-fed dogs are full of energy and love to run and play.

HOW MANY MEALS?

Many dogs can benefit from having their daily food allowance spread over the day, to prevent them from becoming overly hungry while waiting for their next feed. Many Boxer owners are now experiencing the benefits of feeding their dog two, or even three, smaller meals per day rather than one large one, with the realisation that their dogs are less likely to be hanging around the kitchen constantly hoping for something to break their fast which would otherwise last for twenty-four hours.

Tension levels and excitability are also likely to be reduced if a dog is not forced to wait all day before being fed. His digestive system is also less taxed by having to break down

the contents of two smaller meals rather than one large one, which reduces the chances of potentially fatal problems, such as gastric torsion or bloat, occurring.

you should consider changing his diet. Ask your vet for advice. These are the tell-tale signs to watch for:
- Frequent upset stomach
- Wind
- Allergic reactions to external factors such as fleas or grass
- Very smelly, very frequent, large motions
- Under-weight despite eating greedily
- Over-active/under-active
- Eating lots of plants, grass, or sticks
- Eating own faeces.
- Rubbing, chewing or scratching at the base of the tail, feet or abdomen

Exercising your dog

All Boxers love running in the park or through the countryside. In fact, off-lead runs are essential for this energetic breed if they are not to become bored or overweight. The amount of exercise an adult Boxer will need depends on his lifestyle, breeding and fitness level, but a rough guideline is always as much as you can manage.

Boxers have thin coats and generally don't appreciate being hauled out in inclement weather. Of course, this is an advantage when the rain is pouring down outside and you don't much want to go out either. However, just because the body is not keen on getting cold and wet does not mean that the mind can do without exercise – Boxers require more mental stimulation than most dogs, often stretching their owner's imagination and patience to the limit.

Grooming and general care

Grooming is minimal, thanks to the Boxer's short, smooth coat, although it is important to brush or shine the coat with a hound glove or soft chamois as frequently as possible, in order to maintain good handling skills and contact co-operation.

Grooming a Boxer is simple and takes up very little time.

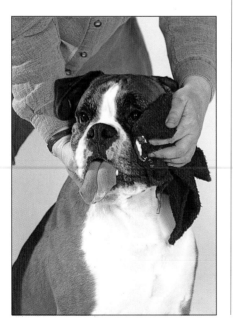

Bathing

It is not necessary to bathe your Boxer frequently. In fact, it is likely to affect the dog's sensitive skin if he is bathed too often. However, Boxers do have a habit of finding indescribable things to roll in when out for walks and many owners prefer to keep both their dogs and their homes smelling sweet and fresh. Persuading a reluctant Boxer to engage in civilised ablutions can be quite a feat; generally a sponge and warm water are sufficient, but for those fool-hardy enough to try the real thing, a large bath tub, a sense of humour and wet-weather gear are recommended!

Boxers hate feeling cold and damp. Whether you have sponged down a dirty dog, or whether he has simply ventured into the garden on a rainy day, it is advisable to ensure that he is completely warm and dry before settling down.

Nail trimming

Many dogs do not appreciate having their nails trimmed, and the art of easy nail clipping is always reliant on a good pair of quality nail clippers and to have accustomed the dog to lots of practice when he was young.

■ Only the tiniest tip of each nail should be removed when cutting nails at home. The blood supply to the nail, the quick, runs through each claw and will bleed profusely if accidentally cut. Such

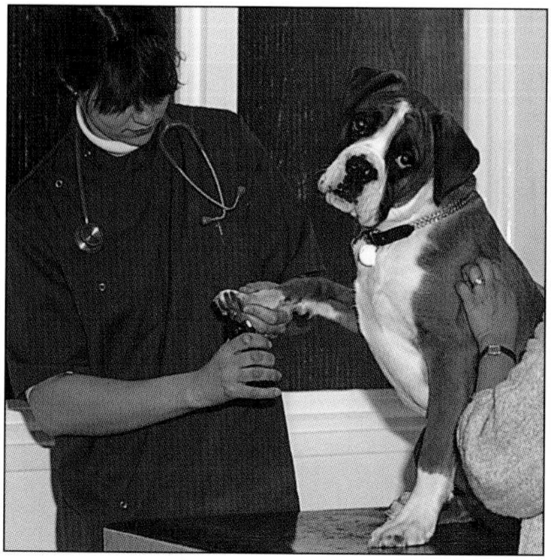

You can take your dog to the vet to have his nails trimmed.

an accident is also likely to make your dog wary of having his nails cut again. It is far better to trim the nails 'little and often' than take off too much at once and risk cutting the quick.

■ The dew claw, sited on the inside of the dog's front 'ankle' needs special attention if it is not to become curved and grow inwards towards the skin. Trimming this claw needs a steady hand and a dog who is happy for you to touch him and handle him all over, ideally when lying down. If in doubt about cutting your dog's nails yourself, ask your vet or a professional dog groomer for help and expert advice.

Checking ears, teeth and eyes

Other aspects of general maintenance should include a regular inspection of the ears. Any brown or smelly discharge indicates an ear infection and should be dealt with promptly by your vet.

■ Teeth should also be inspected, and brushed with a special dog toothpaste and soft brush as often as possible. Dogs build up tartar on their teeth, just like us, and those that are on a soft diet of moist or semi-moist food are particularly susceptible. Tartar and eventual tooth decay result in bad breath as well as discomfort and eating problems for the dog. Tooth brushing is obviously a rather unusual experience for dogs, but most adapt well if it is introduced gently and with plenty of rewards for good behaviour.

You should check and clean your dog's teeth regularly.

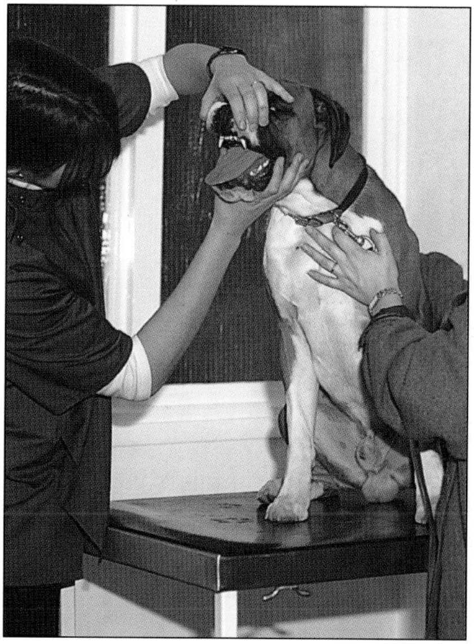

■ Boxers vary in the amount and depth of wrinkling on their faces, but it is important to check that there is no discharge from the eyes and that the skin around the muzzle is dry and clean.

Keeping your dog amused

Many Boxers can be persuaded to enjoy toys and these are a useful addition to the armoury of items required to keep your Boxer amused. However, many dog toys disintegrate as soon as they are chewed, while others lose their novelty value after a couple of days. Ideal toys are ones that are interactive, i.e. they maintain the dog's interest without having to have a human on the other end.

Boxers are prone to separation anxiety; many simply cannot cope with being left at home alone and they are likely to want to chew something to relieve the boredom or frustration of social isolation. Leaving interesting and safe toys for your dog to play with while you are gone is always a wise precaution.

Hollow sterilized bones and hollow rubber toys are ideal, especially if you have the foresight to stuff them full of interesting food morsels, just out of the tongue's reach. These can provide hours of entertainment for your dog, particularly while human company is not available.

Throwing sticks for any dog when

Dogs that are left alone with no toys can become bored and destructive.

outside is not a good idea. Vets have to treat far too many emergency cases every year after sticks have become impaled in dogs' mouths or throats. Wood can also splinter and cause damage to the gut lining. Small balls and chews can be equally hazardous: many dogs suffocate on tennis balls that are too small for them and get stuck in their throats, and some of the larger pieces of flat raw hide chew can also become lodged at the back of the throat, causing suffocation.

Rescue dogs

Unfortunately, there are all too many Boxers awaiting new homes in rescue centres. Many are also cared for by breed rescue societies which try to place dogs with new families if they can no longer live with their original owners. Although many dogs who end up in this situation are simply the innocent victims of financial problems, marriage break-ups and house repossessions, a typical Boxer languishing in a rescue centre is more than likely to be around ten to eighteen months old, and male.

Taking on a rehomed dog is often a good option if you don't wish to have to start from scratch with a new puppy, and you want to give a loving home to a dog who has fallen on hard times. However, it is wise to realise from the outset that only

FAMILY PLANNING

Unless you wish to breed from your dog, it is extremely sensible to have dogs castrated and bitches spayed. This saves an inordinate amount of time chasing your male after he has escaped from your supposedly escape-proof garden, and warding off amorous males from your driveway and protecting your bitch from their advances. In this age with so many dogs needing homes, it is inexcusable to allow either a dog or bitch to produce an unwanted litter. Ask your vet for advice about neutering.

a fortunate minority of people who adopt a rescue dog will find that he is house-trained, sociable with people and other animals and the perfect companion. More often than not, rescue dogs come with their own idiosyncrasies, imperfections and behaviour problems which need time, experience, and a great deal of patience to solve. It is always impossible to know exactly what experiences a dog has had coming from another environment. Some dogs may have suffered neglect, emotional or physical, or abuse, but the majority are simply victims of having been too cute as puppies.

Making your dog feel secure

With these elements in mind, it is perfectly possible to transform a wild 'teenage' Boxer into a sensible good companion, but it does take hard work and commitment. House rules need to be in place from day one. Feeling sorry for the treatment that your dog received in his past may lead initially to some serious errors of judgement. No matter how sorry you feel for your dog,

what he needs now is security.

■ Dogs thrive on routines that are set by their owners. They like to know where they stand in the family – which resources are theirs, what they cannot touch. Many will quickly establish themselves as dictators of your time and, more importantly, your attention, if they are not guided from the beginning. Most rehomed dogs tend to behave beautifully for the first few days or couple of weeks. This is known as the 'honeymoon period' by behaviour counsellors. It is during this time that the dog observes his new family and what goes on in the household on a day-to-day basis. He watches the different members of the family and their interactions with each other. By so doing, he can discover who really rules the roost, who really means what they say, and who is more likely to be a soft-touch for titbits later on.

■ During this time, most dogs are slightly subdued, working on the principle that until they feel more secure in their new environment it is better to keep a low profile and work out the system. Of course, at some stage, the dog is going to begin to feel more secure, and this is when problems are more likely to occur. This is not necessarily a canine take-over bid, but merely a chance to raise objections over the

RESCUE SCHEMES

There are several different breed rescue schemes for Boxers in the UK, as well as all the major rescue centres that care for all breeds. Most will insist that dogs are castrated before being rehomed, and that bitches are spayed as soon as possible. Some even offer voucher schemes which allow for discounts on these operations once you have rehomed the dog. The majority of rescue centres and breed rescue societies will insist on a home visit prior to agreeing to rehome a dog. This is a sensible strategy, ensuring that the prospective owners understand what they are taking on in terms of time, exercise, commitment and expense, as well as making sure that gardens are escape-proof and that the whole family want to be involved in caring for the dog. You can contact the Kennel Club for a list of local breed rescue societies (see page 144).

removal of resources that the dog has been granted over the first few days, or were always granted in his previous home. For example, any dog who has been allowed to lounge full length on the sofa 'because we felt sorry for him', during the first couple of weeks in his new family, is not going to appreciate or understand why the same people now expect him to move off his usual resting place because he has muddy paws.

■ The best advice for the owner of a rehomed dog is to start as you mean to go on. Dogs will never be able to comprehend human follies and inconsistencies. Why should a Boxer appreciate the difference between jumping up at you and being greeted with strokes and friendly words when you are wearing old clothes, and being reprimanded when he does so on the day that you have to wear your best suit to go out to a wedding or meeting.

■ Overall, it is easier to relax a few rules once your new dog has settled in to your home than it is to try to tighten them at a later date. Most Boxers are only too happy to shift out of the way to allow you to cuddle up next to them on the sofa once they feel confident in your relationship with them, but that relationship needs to be built on trust and routine first.

Boarding kennels

Some people who have rehomed a Boxer, particularly those whose dog came via a rescue kennel, are reticent about leaving their dog in boarding kennels when they go away on their holiday. Although it is understandable to worry that your dog will remember his past experiences and become insecure and anxious, it is important to remember that most dogs adapt well to kennel life as a temporary situation.

CHAPTER FIVE

SHOWING YOUR DOG

ENTERING A DOG SHOW

When buying a dog most people look for a companion and family pet. However, for many of us owning a dog brings a degree of pride of ownership and we begin to wonder how well our pet compares with others of the same breed. Many people go to training classes to educate their dog and to ensure that it is properly trained, and there they are bound to meet others who have made a

SHOWS IN YOUR AREA

The breeder from whom you purchased your puppy should be able to give you some indication of the general shows that are held in your area. However, if you are going to take showing seriously you should regularly take one of the weekly dog newspapers that print the advertisements for shows and a list of those for which the entries are closing that particular week. They also provide you with a great deal of information about the show scene and you will find a small section devoted to your breed under the breed notes. The canine press also publish reports of most dog shows, which are written by the judges.

hobby of showing their dog. For most people, showing is just that – an enjoyable hobby – but for many others it can become a consuming passion, even perhaps an obsession. Whatever the strength of your commitment, to get the best out of your dog is time consuming.

Learning about showing

If you are interested in showing your dog, your first step should be to join a breed club. Through its members, its shows, its training days and newsletters, you will quickly pick up the basic requirements of presenting your Boxer to his best advantage. For details of your nearest breed club, you can contact the Kennel Club (see page 144).

The Kennel Club is the ruling body for the world of British dog shows, working trials, field trials, obedience and agility trials. It also runs Cruft's dog show in addition to providing all the rules and regulations that are needed to ensure that showing your dog is as fair as possible.

Showing your dog should be a mutually enjoyable experience.

Types of dog show

There are several types of show in the same way that there are several leagues in the world of soccer.

■ **Championship Shows** are the most prestigious as there are Challenge Certificates available for each breed. The number of Challenge Certificates that are available in any one year is worked out by using a formula that takes into account the number of dogs in that breed being shown. The larger the number of dogs, the more Challenge Certificates are available and vice versa.

However, the number awarded when compared to the number of dogs being shown in the breed is really quite small, and therefore these certificates are important because if a dog can win three of them under different judges he is entitled to be called a champion. Naturally, there is fierce competition at this level.

Championship shows are either general championship shows where most or many of the breeds are scheduled, or

The judge will want to see your dog moving in the ring.

breed championship shows, which are, of course, restricted to one breed only.

■ **Open Shows** are the next level, and many hundreds of these are held each year. These are the shows where you will meet many friends and where your dog will cut his showing teeth. Competition is sometimes quite strong because many breeders and exhibitors use open shows to bring out their young dogs for practice, and sometimes to take their older ones just for a day out even though they have been very successful at championship show level.

■ **Other shows** include Limited Shows, which are restricted to members of a particular society, Sanction Shows, Primary Shows, Matches and Exemption Shows.

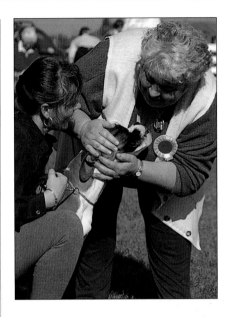

There are many types of dog show, including the highly popular knock-out matches and exemption shows at local level.

Attending a show

Whichever sort of show you attend, the pattern is the same.

1 Firstly, you will need to obtain a schedule and entry form from the Secretary. Most Secretaries prefer you to write in enclosing a stamped addressed envelope, but nowadays many are happy to send you a schedule on receipt of a telephone request. Particularly with the big shows, don't be surprised if you find yourself speaking to an answering machine; the number of enquiries that are received by a Show Secretary as the entries closing date approaches can be many hundreds a day.

2 Having got your schedule, you will need to select the classes that you wish to enter and then complete the entry form, providing all the details that are requested.

3 Of course, your dog will need to be transferred to your name at the Kennel Club, but if the paperwork has not come through you may enter the dog's name with 'TAF' in brackets afterwards. This means 'transfer applied for'. If, for any reason, your dog's name has not yet been accepted by the Kennel Club, you can enter it 'NAF', meaning 'name applied for'.

4 This system is in use for all shows other than primary shows, matches and exemption shows. Entries must be made in advance – sometimes more than two months ahead of the show date. This is to allow the entries to be counted so that sufficient benches and tenting can be arranged and the show catalogues printed, including all the details that you set out on the entry form.

Classes

You will see from the schedule that the breed or variety is divided into various classes. Some have obvious names such as 'Puppy', which is for dogs up to one year old, and 'Junior', which is for dogs up to eighteen months of age, and 'Open', which means that any dog can enter.

THE THRILL OF WINNING

By this time, you will have realised that showing dogs can be an expensive hobby for there is certainly little in the way of prize money to be won. However, everyone who is involved does it for fun and the thrill of winning and, of course, those green Challenge Certificates which allow us to put the title 'Champion' before the name of our dog.

However, the intermediate classes may cause you some confusion. You will find definitions of these classes in the schedule, and, in effect, they mean that if your dog has had a certain amount of wins, he stops being eligible for that particular class. Eligibility is different for

different shows, and therefore you do need to check the schedule to make sure that you have entered in the correct class.

Benching

Larger shows, especially championship shows, are usually benched with the dogs on special trestles which are partitioned off to allow room for each dog to lie down quietly. These days, most smaller shows are not benched and, although benching is expensive, there is no doubt that having to look after your dogs throughout the day and keep them with you wherever you go can sometimes be a bit of a chore. However, most novices have only one dog and therefore it is not really a problem.

Judging

Judges are selected by the show society for their experience and knowledge of the breed, or breeds, that they are judging. Some judges are very good and some, of course, are not so good, although those that judge badly usually do so as a result of incompetence rather than dishonesty!

Successful showing

The secret of success is consistency: no dog ever wins under every judge and few dogs ever lose under every judge. How good your dog is depends largely on how consistent you are. If you usually win or are placed in the top three, then you have almost certainly got a very good

RINGCRAFT

When the time comes for you to enter your class, you should go into the ring and the steward will tell you where to stand. It is very sensible to spend some time watching the other exhibitors so that you have some idea of the procedure when you approach the judge.

■ The judge will usually ask you to come forward and 'stand' your dog. Watch other exhibitors to see how this is done – don't stand at the front of the line in your first class at your first show.

■ The judge will then examine the dog from a distance, look at him probably from the front and the back, approach the dog and check his eyes, teeth, structure and musculature, and the overall conformation.

■ The judge will then ask you to move the dog. Different judges require dogs to move in different ways so watch them carefully and listen to the instructions. After a final look, the judge will move on to the next dog.

dog. If you are usually not considered or left down at the bottom of the line, then, after a period of time, you will have to accept that your dog is not quite as good an example of the breed as you thought he was or would like him to be. The important thing to remember is that whatever the results of the competition you will always take the best dog home – and that's your dog!

PART THREE

HEALTHCARE

In this section on healthcare, there is expert practical advice on how to keep your dog healthy and prevent many common health problems, together with information on canine illnesses and diseases and the special health problems that may affect the Boxer as a breed, especially inherited ones. If you are considering breeding from your Boxer, you will find everything that you need to know about mating, pregnancy, whelping and weaning, and even socializing the puppies. Essential first-aid techniques for use in a wide range of common accidents and emergencies, including road accidents and dog fights, are also featured, with easy-to-follow step-by-step illustrated guides and advice on when you should seek expert veterinary help.

CHAPTER SIX

HEALTH MAINTENANCE

Throughout the health section of this book, where comments relate equally to the dog or the bitch, we have used the term 'he' to avoid the repeated, clumsy use of 'he or she'. Your Boxer is definitely not an 'it'.

SIGNS OF A HEALTHY DOG

- **Appearance**

In general, a healthy dog looks healthy. He wants to play with you, as games are a very important part of a dog's life. A Boxer, especially, is always ready for his walk.

- **Eyes and nose**

His eyes are bright and alert, and, apart from the small amount of 'sleep' in the inner corners, there is no discharge. His nose is usually cold and wet with no discharge, although a little clear fluid can be normal. A Boxer is a 'brachycephalic' dog — one with a short head and nose.

- **Ears**

His ears are also alert and very responsive to sounds around him. In the Boxer, the ear flaps (pinnae) are usually folded over forwards. The inside of his ear flap is pale pink in appearance and silky in texture. No wax will be visible and there will be no unpleasant smell. He will not scratch his ears much, nor shake his head excessively.

- **Coat**

A healthy Boxer's coat will be short, glossy and feel pleasant to the touch. He will not scratch excessively and scurf will be not be present. His coat will smell 'doggy' but not unpleasant, and he will probably shed hairs (moult) continuously to some degree, especially if he lives indoors with the family.

- **Tail**

A Boxer's tail, if left undocked at the natural length, will taper gradually to the tip. If docked, as has been the custom, the remaining length will be short — about 2.5 – 5 cm (1 – 2 in).

- **Teeth**

The teeth of a healthy dog should be white and smooth. If they are yellow and dull there may be plaque or tartar formation. As in many brachycephalic breeds, the lower jaw will usually be a little longer than the upper jaw so that the lower incisor teeth (and often the canines) protrude in front of the upper ones. This 'undershot jaw' is normal in the Boxer.

- **Claws and feet**

A dog's claws should not be broken nor too long. There is a short non-sensitive tip, as in our nails. The claw should end at the ground, level with the pad. Dogs will not pay much attention to their feet, apart from normal washing, but excessive licking can indicate disease. Boxers are born with five toes on the front feet, with one in our 'thumb' position called the dew claw, and four on the hind feet. If a puppy is born with a dew claw on a hind foot, it is usually removed at three to five days of age as they become pendulous and are often injured as an adult. It has been customary to remove front dew claws in Boxer pups, but this is optional.

- **Stools and urination**

A healthy dog will pass stools between once and six times a day depending on diet,

POINTS OF THE DOG

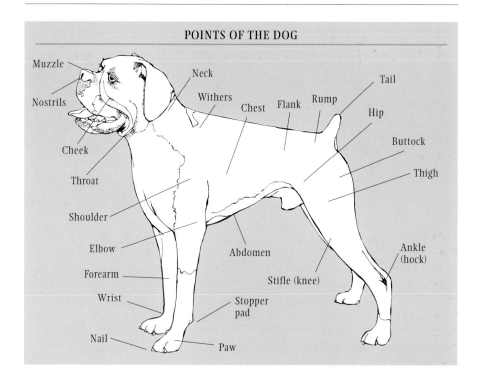

Muzzle
Neck
Tail
Nostrils
Withers
Chest
Flank
Rump
Hip
Cheek
Buttock
Throat
Thigh
Shoulder
Elbow
Abdomen
Ankle (hock)
Forearm
Stifle (knee)
Wrist
Stopper pad
Nail
Paw

temperament, breed and opportunity. A male dog will urinate numerous times on a walk as this is territorial behaviour. Bitches usually urinate less often.

■ **Weight**

A healthy dog will look in good bodily condition for his size — not too fat and not too thin. Sixty per cent of dogs nowadays are overweight, so balance the diet with the right amount of exercise.

■ **Feeding**

A dog will usually be ready for his meal and once adult, he should be fed regularly at the same time each day. Most dogs require one meal a day, but some healthy dogs seem to require two meals daily just to maintain a normal weight. These are the very active dogs who tend to 'burn off' more calories.

DIET

■ **Feeding a puppy**

The correct diet as a pup is essential to allow him to achieve his full potential during the growing phase. In a Boxer this is up to eighteen months to two years of age. Many home-made diets are deficient in various ingredients just because owners do not fully appreciate the balance that is required. It is far better to rely on one of the correctly formulated and prepared commercial diets which will contain the correct amounts and proportions of essential nutrients, such as protein, carbohydrates, fats, roughage, minerals, such as calcium and phosphorus, and essential vitamins.

Modern thinking is that the complete,

dried, extruded diets available now have so many advantages that the new puppy could be put on to a 'growth' formula diet of this type from as early as four weeks. Crunchy diets such as these have advantages in dental care also.

However, there are some excellent canned and semi-moist diets available but care should be taken to check whether these are complete diets, or complementary foods which require biscuits and other ingredients to be added. If

CARE OF THE OLDER DOG

Provided that he has been well cared for throughout his life, there may be no need to treat the older Boxer any differently as old age approaches. Boxers do not usually live as long as most other breeds, and although we have seen many a Boxer of eleven years or more, nine years is a reasonable life expectancy for this breed.

■ **Diet**
This should be chosen to:
■ Improve existing problems
■ Slow or prevent the development of disease
■ Enable the dog to maintain his ideal body weight
■ Be highly palatable and digestible
■ Contain an increased amount of fatty acids, vitamins (especially A, B and E) and certain minerals, notably zinc
■ Contain reduced amounts of protein, phosphorus and sodium

■ **Fitness and exercise**
A healthy Boxer should hardly need to reduce his exercise until he is eight or nine years old. There should be no sudden change in routine; a sudden increase in exercise is as wrong as a sudden drop. Let the dog tell you when he has had enough. If he lags behind, has difficulty in walking, breathing or getting to his feet after a long walk, then

it is time to consider a health check. As dogs age, they need a good diet, company, comfort and a change of scenery to add interest to their lives.

■ **Avoiding obesity**
■ As the body ages, all body systems age with it. The heart and circulation, lungs, muscles and joints are not as efficient as they used to be. These should all be able to support and transport a dog of the correct weight but may fail if the dog is grossly overweight.
■ A dog of normal weight will approach old age with a greater likelihood of reaching it. It is wise to diet your dog at this stage if you have let his weight increase. Food intake can be increased almost to normal when the weight loss has been achieved.
■ Reduce the calorie intake to about sixty per cent of normal, to encourage the conversion of body fat back into energy. Feed a high-fibre diet so that the dog does not feel hungry. Maintenance levels of essential nutrients, such as protein, vitamins and minerals, must be provided so that deficiencies do not occur.
■ Your veterinary surgeon will be able to supply or advise on the choice of several prescription low-calorie diets which are available in both dried and canned form, or instruct you on how to mix your own.

you really know your diets, it is of course possible to formulate a home-prepared diet from fresh ingredients.

Your Boxer should be fed four times a day until he is three months of age, and with a complete dried food this can be left down so that he can help himself to food whenever he feels hungry. The exact amount of food will depend on his age and the type of food, and if instructions are not included on the packet, you should consult your vet.

At three months of age, he should be fed three times daily, but each meal should have more in it. By six months of age, he could be down to two larger meals a day, still of a puppy or growth-formula food. He should remain on this type of food until he is twelve to eighteen months of age, and then change to an adult maintenance version.

■ **Feeding an adult dog**

Adult dogs can be fed on any one of the excellent range of quality dog foods now available. Your vet is the best person to advise you as to the best diet for your Boxer, and this advice will vary depending on his age, amount of exercise and condition.

■ **Feeding an older dog**

From the age of eight or nine years onwards, your Boxer may benefit from a change to a diet specially formulated for the older dog, as he will have differing requirements as his body organs age. Your vet is the best person with whom to discuss this, as he will be able to assess your dog's general condition and requirements.

EXERCISE

As a puppy, your Boxer should not be given too much exercise. At the age that you acquire him, usually six to eight weeks of age, he will need gentle, frequent forays into your garden, or other people's gardens provided they are not open to stray dogs. He can and should meet other vaccinated, reliable dogs or puppies and play with them. He will also enjoy energetic games with you, but remember that in any tug-of-war type contest you should win!

■ **Exercise and vaccinations**

Although you should be taking him out with you to accustom him to the sights and sounds of normal life, at this stage you should not put him down on the ground in public places until the vaccination course is completed, because of the risk of infection.

■ **Exercise after vaccinations**

About a week after his second vaccination, you will be able to take him out for walks, but remember that at this stage he is equivalent to a toddler. His bones have not calcified, his joints are still developing, and too much strenuous exercise can affect normal development. This applies especially to lively and fairly large breeds with rapid growth like Boxers, which at this stage may be gaining up to 1.5 kg (3 lb) a week. Perhaps three walks daily for about half an hour each is ample by about four months of age, rising to two to three hours by the time he reaches six months. At this stage, as his bones and joints develop, he could then be taken for more vigorous runs in the country. However, he should not be involved in really tiring exercise until he is nine months to a year old, by which time his joints have almost fully matured, and his bones have fully calcified.

■ **Exercising an adult dog**

As an adult dog, his exercise tolerance will be almost limitless, certainly better than most of us! It is essential that such a lively, active, intelligent breed as the Boxer has an adequate amount of exercise daily — it is not really sufficient to provide exercise just at weekends. A daily quota of one to two hours of interesting, energetic exercise is essential. As the Boxer is usually an investigative, self-willed breed, rarely content to stay close to you on a walk and wandering off from time to time, it is essential that he is well trained to respond to your commands. During exercise Boxers enjoy playing games, so try to exercise his brain as well as his body.

DAILY CARE

There are several things that you should be doing daily for your dog to keep him in first-class condition.

■ **Grooming**

All dogs benefit from a daily grooming. Use a stiff brush or comb obtained from your vet or pet shop, and ensure you specify that it is for a Boxer as brushes vary. Comb or brush in the direction of the lie of the hair. Hair is

constantly growing and being shed, especially in dogs that live indoors with us, as their bodies become confused as to which season it is in a uniformly warm house. Brushing removes dead hair and scurf, and stimulates the sebaceous glands to produce the natural oils that keep the coat glossy.

■ **Bathing**

Dogs should not require frequent baths, but can benefit from a periodic shampoo using a dog shampoo with a conditioner included.

■ **Feeding**

Dogs do not benefit from a frequently changed diet. Their digestive systems seem to get used to a regular diet; dogs do not worry if they have the same food every day — that is a human trait — so establish a complete nutritious diet that your dog enjoys and stick to it. Boxers rarely have digestive problems but a regular established daily diet is one way of ensuring this.

The day's food should be given at a regular time each day. Usually the adult dog

VACCINATIONS

Vaccination is the administration of a modified live, or killed, form of an infection which does not cause illness in the dog, but instead stimulates the formation of antibodies against the disease itself. There are four major diseases against which all dogs should be vaccinated. These are:
■ Canine distemper (also called hardpad)
■ Infectious canine hepatitis
■ Leptospirosis
■ Canine parvovirus
Many vaccination courses now include a component against parainfluenza virus, one of the causes of kennel cough, that scourge

of boarding and breeding kennels. A separate vaccine against bordetella, another cause of kennel cough, can be given in droplet form down the nose prior to your dog entering boarding kennels. All these diseases are described in the following chapter (see page 105).

■ **Vaccinating puppies**

In the puppy, vaccination should start at eight to ten weeks of age, and is a course of two injections, two to four weeks apart. It is recommended that adult dogs have an annual check up and booster inoculation by the vet.

TEETH AND JAWS

The molars crush the food whereas the incisors (smaller front teeth) are used for scraping. The large, pointed canine teeth are used for tearing meat.

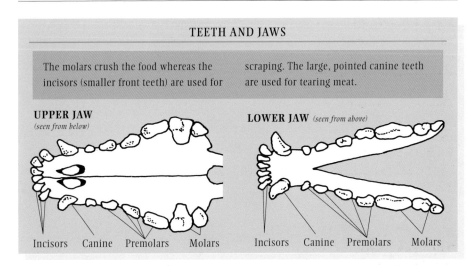

UPPER JAW *(seen from below)*

Incisors   Canine   Premolars   Molars

LOWER JAW *(seen from above)*

Incisors   Canine   Premolars   Molars

will have one meal a day, at either breakfast time or teatime. Both are equally acceptable but, ideally, hard exercise should not be given within an hour of a full meal. It is better to give your dog a long walk and then feed him on your return. Some dogs seem to like two smaller meals a day, and this is perfectly acceptable, provided that the total amount of food given is not excessive.

■ **Water**
Your dog should have a full bowl of clean, fresh water changed once or twice a day, and this should be permanently available. This is particularly important if he is on a complete dried food.

■ **Toileting**
Your dog should be let out into the garden first thing in the morning to toilet, and this can be taught quite easily on command and in a specified area of the garden. You should not take the dog out for a walk to toilet, unless you just do not have the space at home. The mess should be in your premises and then picked up and flushed down the toilet daily. Other people, children in particular, should

not have to put up with our dogs' mess.

Throughout the day he should have access to a toileting area every few hours, and always last thing at night before you all turn in. Dogs will usually want to, and can be conditioned to, defecate immediately after a meal, so this should be encouraged.

■ **Company**
Boxers are very sociable dogs and require lots of exercise and mental stimulation. There is no point in having one unless you intend to be there most of the time. Obviously a well-trained and socialized adult should be capable of being left for one to three hours at a time, but puppies need constant attention if they are to grow up well balanced. Games, as mentioned before, are an essential daily pastime.

■ **Dental care**
Some complete diets are very crunchy; for example, by mimicking the wild dog's (e.g. fox or wolf) diet of a whole rabbit (bones, fur etc.), you will keep the teeth relatively free of plaque and tartar. However, a daily teeth inspection is sensible. Lift the lips and look at not only the front incisor and canine teeth but

also the back premolars and molars. They should be a healthy, shiny white like ours.

If not, or if on a soft, canned or fresh meat diet, daily brushing using a toothbrush and enzyme toothpaste is advisable. Hide chew sticks help to clean teeth, as do root vegetables, such as carrots, and many vets recommend a large raw marrow bone. These can, however, occasionally cause teeth to break. Various manufacturers have brought out tasty, chewy food items that benefit teeth, and your vet will be able to recommend a suitable one.

Pups are born with, or acquire shortly after birth, a full set of temporary teeth. These start to be shed at about sixteen weeks of age with the central incisors, and the transition from temporary to permanent teeth should be complete by six months of age. If extra teeth seem to be present, or if teeth seem out of position at this age, it is wise to see your vet.

■ General inspection

A full inspection by you is not necessary on a daily basis, unless you notice something different about your dog. However, it is as well to cast your eyes over him to ensure that the coat and skin are in good order, his eyes are bright and his ears are clean, and he is not lame. Check that he has eaten his food, and that his stools and urine look normal.

PERIODIC HEALTHCARE

Worming

■ Roundworms (Toxocara)

All puppies should be wormed fortnightly from two weeks to three months of age, and then monthly until they are six months of age. Thereafter in a male or neutered female Boxer, you should worm twice yearly. Dogs used for

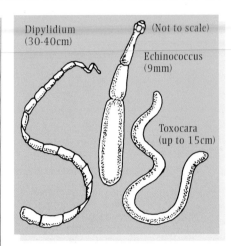

Dipylidium (30-40cm)

Echinococcus (9mm)

Toxocara (up to 15cm)

(Not to scale)

breeding have special roundworming requirements and you should consult your vet about them. There is evidence that entire females undergoing false (pseudo) pregnancies have roundworm larvae migrating in their tissues, so they should be wormed at this important time.

■ Tapeworms (Dipylidium and Echinococcus)

These need intermediate hosts (fleas and usually sheep offal respectively) to complete their life cycle, so prevention of contact with these is advisable. As a precaution, most vets recommend tapeworming adult dogs twice a year.

Note: there are very effective and safe combined round and tape wormers available now from your vet.

SPECIAL HEALTH PROBLEMS

The Boxer is usually a fit, friendly and interesting companion. There are, however, some health problems that are known to occur in this breed particularly. A few of the more common problems are detailed here.

■ **Hyperplastic gingivitis**

This is an unusual condition in which the gums begin to enlarge and spread down the teeth, often resulting in the teeth being enveloped. This can be painful as the dog will bite on the gum, and surgery is necessary to correct it. The first sign to the owner may be a fetid odour from the mouth. Recurrence is common.

■ **Epulis**

This is similar to the above condition, but is often a single mass of gum overgrowth forming a discrete tumour-like lesion. Surgical removal is usually straightforward.

■ **Spondylitis deformans**

This is a type of arthritis occurring in mid to late life in the spinal column. New areas of abnormal bone form, usually on the base of the vertebrae, and gradually fuse the bones of the spine together. It usually occurs in the mid back, and the signs are those of pain and unwillingness to climb stairs, and often inability to settle down.

Diagnosis: X-rays and clinical signs in a dog of the right age.

Treatment: anti-inflammatory tablets or injections can often help.

■ **Progressive axonopathy**

This is a degenerative disease of the peripheral nerves (not the brain and spinal cord). It is an inherited disease of the Boxer. There is no treatment available.

■ **Cardiomyopathy**

This is seen more commonly in the Boxer than many other breeds. The heart becomes enlarged and the heart muscle is weak. It results in the dog being breathless, and not able to enjoy exercise. Fainting will sometimes occur, often following a coughing bout (see First Aid, page 134). Congestive heart failure is often the end result.

Diagnosis: clinical examination by the vet, and often an ECG and X-rays.

Treatment: various heart drugs are helpful in this condition.

■ **Aortic stenosis**

This is a deformity in the aortic heart valve. It often causes no symptoms, but sudden death can and does occur.

Diagnosis: a heart murmur is heard by the vet through the stethoscope; X-rays may help as will an ultrasound examination of the heart.

Treatment: surgical treatment is not feasible, and medical treatment is of limited value.

■ **Corneal recurrent erosion**

This does seem to be a special problem in Boxers. A scratch or other injury to the cornea on the front of the eye will invariably heal with medical treatment in most breeds, but not always in the Boxer. In our experience, surgical intervention is usually necessary and, despite complete healing, the problem has a tendency to recur.

Diagnosis: fluorescine eye drops will show up the ulcer in the cornea.

Treatment: antibiotic ointments or drops may help, but often an operation to suture the third eyelid to the upper lid is needed. This provides a blood supply which heals the ulcer.

Note: in addition to the specific advice given above, you can reduce the chances of your new dog having these problems by asking the right questions about his ancestry before you purchase him.

CHAPTER SEVEN

DISEASES AND ILLNESSES

RESPIRATORY DISEASES

■ Rhinitis

This infection of the nose, which is caused by viruses, bacteria or fungi, is sometimes seen in the Boxer. It may also be part of a disease such as distemper or kennel cough. Sneezing or a clear or coloured discharge are the usual signs.

Another cause, due to the dog's habit of sniffing, is a grass seed or other foreign object inhaled through the nostrils. The dog starts to sneeze violently, often after a walk through long grass.

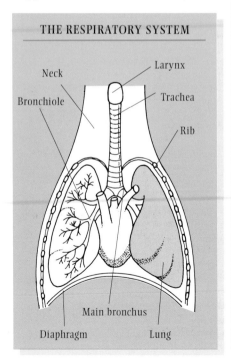

THE RESPIRATORY SYSTEM

Neck

Larynx

Bronchiole

Trachea

Rib

Main bronchus

Diaphragm

Lung

■ Tumours of the nose

These do occur in the Boxer. The first sign is often haemorrhage from one nostril. X-rays reveal a mass in the nasal chamber.

Diseases producing a cough

A cough is a reflex which clears foreign matter from the bronchi, trachea and larynx. Severe inflammation of these structures will also stimulate the cough reflex.

■ Laryngitis, tracheitis and bronchitis

Inflammation of these structures can be caused by an infection, such as kennel cough or canine distemper, by irritant fumes or by foreign material. Usually, all three parts of the airway are affected at the same time.

Bronchitis is a major problem in the older dog, caused by a persistent infection or an irritation, producing irreversible changes in the bronchi. A cough develops and increases until the dog seems to cough constantly.

Diseases producing laboured breathing

Laboured breathing is normally caused by those diseases that occupy space within the chest, and reduce the lung tissue available for oxygenation of the blood. An X-ray produces an accurate diagnosis.

■ Pneumonia

This is an infection of the lungs. It is uncommon in the Boxer but can occur, caused by viruses, bacteria, fungi or foreign material.

■ Chest tumours

These can cause respiratory problems by

INFECTIOUS DISEASES

- **Distemper (hardpad)**

This is a frequently fatal virus disease which usually affects dogs under one year of age. Affected dogs cough and have a discharge from the eyes and nose. Pneumonia often develops, and vomiting and diarrhoea usually follow. If the dog lives, nervous symptoms such as fits, paralysis, or chorea (a type of regular twitch) are likely. The pads of the feet become thickened and hard — hence the other name for the disease, hardpad. **Treatment:** antibiotics sometimes help, but the only real answer is prevention by vaccination as a puppy, and annual boosters.

- **Infectious canine hepatitis**

This affects the liver. In severe cases, the first sign may be a dog completely off his food, very depressed and collapsed. Some die suddenly. Recovery is unlikely from this severe form of the disease. Prevention by vaccination is essential.

- **Leptospirosis**

Two separate diseases affect dogs. Both, in addition to causing severe and often fatal disease in the dog, are infectious to humans.

- **Leptospira canicola** causes acute kidney disease.

- **Leptospira icterohaemorrhagiae**

causes an acute infection of the liver, often leading to jaundice.
Treatment of both is often unsuccessful, and prevention by vaccination is essential.

- **Canine parvovirus**

This affects the bowels, causing a sudden onset of vomiting and diarrhoea, often with blood, and severe depression. As death is usually due to dehydration, prompt replacement of the fluid and electrolyte loss is essential. In addition, antibiotics are also usually given to prevent secondary bacterial infection. Prevention by vaccination is essential.

- **Kennel cough**

This is a highly infectious cough occurring mainly in kennelled dogs. There are two main causes:
- Bordetella, a bacterial infection
- Parainfluenza virus

Both affect the trachea and lungs. Occasionally, a purulent discharge from the nose and eyes may develop. Antibiotics and rest are usually prescribed by the vet. Prevention of both by vaccination is recommended.

---

occupying lung space and by causing the accumulation of fluid within the chest.

Accidents

Respiratory failure commonly follows accidents. Several types of injury may be seen:
- **Haemorrhage into the lung (Haemothorax)**

Rupture of a blood vessel in the lung will release blood which then fills the air sacs.

- **Free air in the chest (Pneumothorax)**

A ruptured lung allows air to surround the lungs and then causes severe respiratory problems in the affected dog.

- **Ruptured diaphragm**

This allows abdominal organs, such as the liver, spleen or stomach, to move forward into the chest cavity.

HEART AND CIRCULATION DISEASES

Heart attack

In the human sense, heart attack is uncommon. Collapse or fainting, however, does occur in Boxers due to inadequate cardiac function (see First Aid, page 134).
- **Cardiomyopathy and Aortic stenosis** (See Special problems of the Boxer, page 103.)

Heart murmurs

- Acquired disease may result from wear and tear or inflammation of heart valves, problems of rhythm and rate, or disease of the heart muscle.
- Signs of disease may include weakness, lethargy, panting, cough, abdominal

SIGNS OF HEART FAILURE

These may include the following:
- Exercise intolerance
- Lethargy
- Panting and/or cough
- Enlargement of the abdomen due to fluid accumulation
- Poor digestion and weight loss

Veterinary investigation involves thorough examination, possibly X-rays of the chest, ECG and, in some cases, ultrasound scanning.

distension, collapse and weight loss.
- **Congenital heart disease** is usually due to valve defects or a hole in the heart.

THE CIRCULATORY SYSTEM

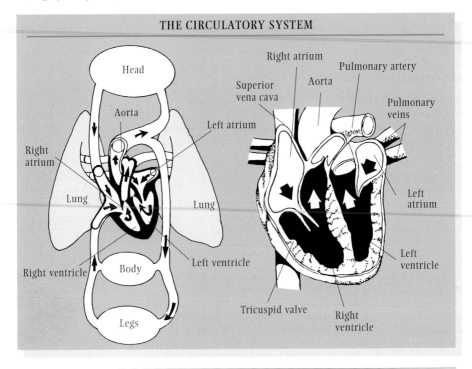

Signs of disease may include the sudden death of a pup, or weakness and failure to thrive or grow at a normal rate.
Note: congestive heart failure is the end result of any of these defects.

Heart block

This is an acquired problem. A nerve impulse conduction failure occurs in the specialized heart muscle responsible for maintaining normal rhythm and rate.

Blood clotting defects

- **Clotting problems** may result from poisoning with Warfarin rat poison. Haemorrhage then occurs which requires immediate treatment (see First Aid, page 132).
- **Congenital clotting defects** arise if the pup is born with abnormal blood platelets or clotting factors, both of which are essential in normal clotting. von Willebrand's disease is a platelet disorder found occasionally in Boxers.

Tumours

The spleen, which is a reservoir for blood, is a relatively common site for tumours, especially in older dogs. Splenic tumours can bleed slowly into the abdomen or rupture suddenly, causing collapse. Surgical removal of the spleen is necessary

DIGESTIVE SYSTEM DISEASES

Mouth problems

Dental disease
- **Dental tartar** forms on the tooth surfaces when left-over food (plaque) solidifies on the

teeth. This irritates the adjacent gum, causing pain, mouth odour, gum recession and, ultimately, tooth loss. This inevitable progression to periodontal disease may be prevented if plaque is removed by regular tooth brushing coupled with good diet, large chews and hard biscuits.

- **Periodontal disease** is inflammation and erosion of the gums around the tooth roots. Careful scaling and polishing of the teeth by your vet under an anaesthetic is necessary to save the teeth.
- **Dental caries** (tooth decay) is common in people, but not so in dogs *unless they are given chocolate and other sweet foods.*
- **Tooth fractures** can result from trauma in road accidents or if your dog is an enthusiastic stone chewer.
- **Epulis and Hyperplastic gingivitis** are benign overgrowths of the gums. Surgical removal is needed (see Special problems of the Boxer, page 103).

Salivary cysts

These may occur as swellings under the tongue or neck, resulting from a ruptured salivary duct.

Mouth tumours

These are often highly malignant, growing rapidly and spreading to other organs. First symptoms may be bad breath, increased salivation, and bleeding from the mouth plus difficulties in eating.
- **Foreign bodies in the mouth** (See First Aid, page 137.)

Problems causing vomiting

- **Gastritis**
This is inflammation of the stomach and can

result from unsuitable diet, scavenging or infection. The dog repeatedly vomits either food or yellowish fluid and froth, which may be blood stained.

■ **Obstruction of the oesophagus**
This leads to regurgitation of food immediately after feeding, and may be caused by small bones or other foreign bodies. Diagnosis is confirmed by X-ray or examination with an endoscope, and treatment must not be delayed.

■ **Obstruction lower down the gut, in the stomach or intestine**
This may result from items such as stones and corks etc. Tumours can also lead to obstructive vomiting. The dog rapidly becomes very ill and the diagnosis is usually confirmed by palpation, X-rays or exploratory surgery.

■ **Intussusception**
This is telescoping of the bowel which can follow diarrhoea, especially in puppies. Surgery is essential.

■ **Gastric dilation**
(See First Aid, page 138.)

Pancreatic diseases

■ **Acute pancreatitis**
This is an extremely painful and serious condition requiring intensive therapy. It can be life-threatening.

■ **Diabetes mellitus**
Another function of the pancreas is to manufacture the hormone insulin, which controls blood sugar levels. If insulin is deficient, blood and urine glucose levels rise, both of which can be detected in laboratory

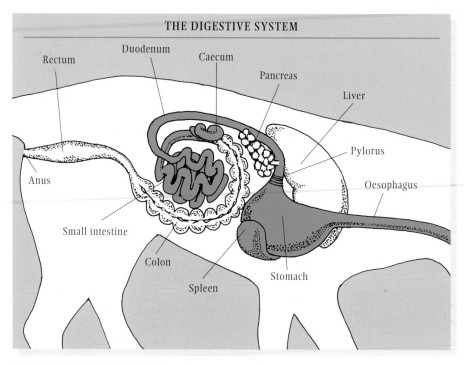

THE DIGESTIVE SYSTEM

Rectum · Duodenum · Caecum · Pancreas · Liver · Pylorus · Oesophagus · Anus · Small intestine · Colon · Spleen · Stomach

PROBLEMS CAUSING DIARRHOEA

■ **Dietary diarrhoea**
This can occur as a result of sudden changes in diet, scavenging, feeding unsuitable foods or stress (especially in pups when they go to their new home).

■ **Enteritis**
This is inflammation of the small intestines which can be caused by infection, e.g. parvovirus, a severe worm burden or food poisoning. Continued diarrhoea leads to dehydration.
Treatment: treat the original cause, and give a light diet of fish, chicken, scrambled eggs or a veterinary prescription diet until the stools are normal.

■ **Colitis**
This is inflammation of the large bowel (colon), and symptoms include straining and frequent defecation, watery faeces with mucous or blood, and often an otherwise healthy dog. This is a problem that is frequently encountered in the Boxer and you should seek veterinary advice.
Treatment: treat the original cause, and give your Boxer a light diet of fish, chicken, scrambled eggs or a veterinary prescription diet until the stools are normal. It may even be necessary to change your dog's diet permanently.

■ **Tumours of the bowel**
These are more likely to cause vomiting than diarrhoea, but one called lymphosarcoma causes diffuse thickening of the gut lining which may lead to diarrhoea.

---

testing. Affected animals have an increased appetite and thirst, weight loss and lethargy. If left untreated, the dog may go into a diabetic coma.

■ **Pancreatic tumours**
These are relatively common and are usually highly malignant. Symptoms vary from vomiting, weight loss and signs of abdominal pain to acute jaundice. The prognosis is usually hopeless, and death rapidly occurs.

LIVER DISEASES

■ **Acute hepatitis**
Infectious canine hepatitis and leptospirosis (see Infectious diseases, page 105). They are not common as most dogs are vaccinated.

■ **Chronic liver failure**
This can be due to heart failure, tumours or cirrhosis. Affected dogs usually lose weight and become depressed, go off their food and may vomit. Diarrhoea and increased thirst are other possible symptoms. The liver may increase or decrease in size, and there is sometimes fluid retention in the abdomen. Jaundice is sometimes apparent. Diagnosis of liver disease depends on symptoms, blood tests, X-rays or ultrasound examination, and possibly liver biopsy.

SKIN DISEASES

Itchy skin diseases

Parasites
■ **Fleas** are the commonest cause of skin disease, and dogs often become allergic to them. They are dark, fast-moving, sideways-flattened insects, about 2 mm (1/8 in) long. They spend about two hours a day feeding on

STRUCTURE OF THE SKIN

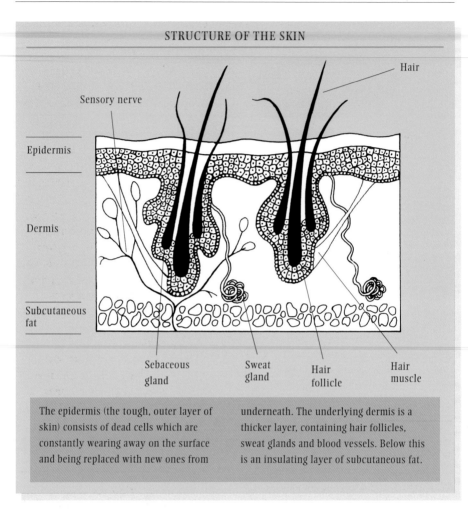

The epidermis (the tough, outer layer of skin) consists of dead cells which are constantly wearing away on the surface and being replaced with new ones from underneath. The underlying dermis is a thicker layer, containing hair follicles, sweat glands and blood vessels. Below this is an insulating layer of subcutaneous fat.

the dog, and then jump off and spend the rest of the day breeding and laying eggs. They live for about three weeks and can lay twenty eggs a day. Thus each flea may leave behind 400 eggs which hatch out in as little as three weeks. It is important to treat the dog and the environment, e.g. his bedding etc.

■ **Lice** are small, whitish insects which crawl very slowly between and up the hairs. They lay eggs on the hair, spend their entire life on the dog and are less common and much easier to treat than fleas.

■ **Mange** is caused by a mite (Sarcoptes) which burrows into the skin, causing intense irritation and hair loss. It is very contagious and more common in young dogs. It also spends its entire life on the dog.

■ **Bacterial infections**
These are common in the dog and are often secondary to some other skin disease, such as

TUMOURS AND CYSTS

■ **Sebaceous cysts**
These are round, painless nodules in the skin and vary from 2 mm ($^1/_8$ in) up to 4 cm (1$^1/_2$ in) in diameter. They are common in the Boxer.

■ **Warts**
These are quite common in the older dog.

■ **Fibromas**
Together with other benign skin tumours, these do occur commonly in the older Boxer to such a degree that they are often referred to as 'Boxer lumps'. They are not life-threatening but if they become too large, they should be surgically removed.

■ **Anal adenomas**
These frequently develop around the anus in old male dogs. They ulcerate when they are quite small and produce small bleeding points.

mange or allergies. Consult your vet.

■ **Folliculitis**
This is a common skin infection in Boxers. It is a bacterial infection of the hair follicles, and is seen as itchy red pustules with a central hair. If untreated it can lead to:

■ **Pyoderma**
This can be an acute, wet, painful area of the skin (wet eczema), or a more persistent infection appearing as ring-like sores. Both are quite common in the Boxer.

■ **Furunculosis**
This is a deeper, more serious infection, which is seen quite often in the Boxer.

Treatment: all three bacterial infections

will require a long course of antibiotics.

■ **Contact dermatitis**
This is an itchy reddening of the skin, usually of the abdomen, groin, armpit or feet, where the hair is thinnest and less protective. It can be an allergic response to materials, such as wool, nylon or carpets, or to a direct irritant, such as oil, or a disinfectant.

■ **Urticaria**
This is seen as the rapid sudden development of itchy lumps in the skin all over the body. It is an allergic response to something that the dog has eaten, breathed in or contacted and seems to occur more often in Boxers than other breeds. It is easily seen as the hairs stand up, but can occur on the face, above the eyes or in the ears when it is very apparent. The condition is easily reversed by an antihistamine injection, but will sometimes resolve spontaneously.

■ **Lick granuloma**
This is a thickened, hairless patch of skin on the front of the wrist or the side of the ankle seen quite often in the Boxer. It results from constant licking of this area because of boredom or neurosis.

Non-itchy skin diseases

■ **Demodectic mange**
This is caused by a congenitally-transmitted parasitic mite and is seen usually in growing dogs. It causes non-itchy patchy hair loss. It is quite difficult to treat.

■ **Ticks**
These are parasitic spiders resembling small grey peas that attach themselves to the skin. They drop off after a week, but should be removed when noticed. Soak them with surgical spirit and pull them out using fine tweezers.

PARASITES

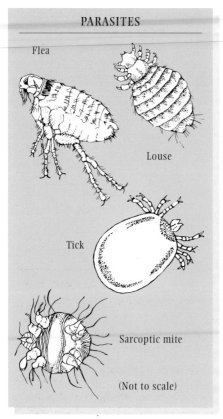

Flea

Louse

Tick

Sarcoptic mite

(Not to scale)

- **Ringworm**
This is a fungal infection of the hairs and skin causing bald patches. It is transmissible to man.
- **Hormonal skin disease**
This patchy, symmetrical hair loss, usually on the flanks, is common in the Boxer. Blood tests are necessary for an exact diagnosis, but a thyroid hormone deficiency is a cause.

DISEASES OF THE ANAL AREA

- **Anal sac impaction**
This is very common. The anal sacs are scent glands and are little used in the dog.

If the secretion slowly accumulates in the gland instead of being emptied during defecation, the overfull anal sac becomes itchy. The dog drags his anus along the ground or bites himself around the base of his tail. Unless the sacs are emptied by your vet, an abscess may form.

DISEASES OF THE FEET

- **Interdigital eczema**
Dogs readily lick their feet after minor damage, and this makes the feet very wet. Infection then occurs between the pads.
- **Interdigital cysts and abscesses**
These are painful swellings between the toes which may make the dog lame. In most cases, the cause is unknown, but sometimes they can be caused by a grass seed penetrating the skin between the toes.
- **Foreign body in the pad**
The most common foreign body is a sharp

STRUCTURE OF THE FOOT

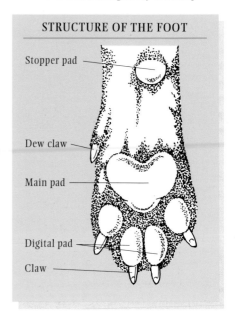

Stopper pad

Dew claw

Main pad

Digital pad

Claw

fragment of glass, or a thorn. The dog is usually very lame and the affected pad is painful to the touch. Often an entry point will be seen on the pad.

■ **Nail bed infections**
The toe becomes swollen and painful and the dog lame. The bone may become diseased and this can lead to amputation of the affected toe.

EAR DISEASES

Haematoma

This is a painless, sometimes large, blood blister in the ear flap, usually caused by head shaking due to an ear infection or irritation.

Infection (Otitis)

This is due to his fairly hair-free ear flap, and good ventilation of the ear. The Boxer is not particularly prone to ear infections. When otitis occurs, a smelly discharge appears, and the dog shakes his head or scratches his ear.

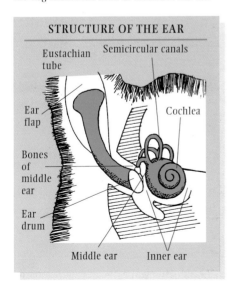

STRUCTURE OF THE EAR

Eustachian tube · Semicircular canals · Ear flap · Cochlea · Bones of middle ear · Ear drum · Middle ear · Inner ear

If the inner ear is affected, the dog may also show a head tilt or a disturbance in his balance.

■ **Treatment:** antibiotic ear drops are usually successful, but sometimes a surgical operation is needed. The vet must be consulted as there are several possible reasons for ear disease including ear mites and grass seeds.

EYE DISEASES

Prolapse of the eye

(See First Aid, page 137.)

Conjunctivitis

This is common in the dog. The white of the eye appears red and discharges. Possible causes include viruses, bacteria, chemicals, allergies, trauma or foreign bodies.

Keratitis

This is a very sore inflammation of the cornea which may appear blue and lose its shiny appearance.

Corneal ulcer

This is an erosion of part of the surface of the cornea and can follow an injury or keratitis.

Corneal recurrent erosion

This is a sequel to the above and does seem to be a special problem in Boxers. Surgical intervention is usually necessary and, despite complete healing, the problem has a tendency to recur (see Special problems of the Boxer, page 103).

THE EYE

Light rays pass through the cornea and pupil, and are focused by the lens on to the retina. They are then converted into nerve impulses and passed via the optic nerve to the visual cortex of the brain.

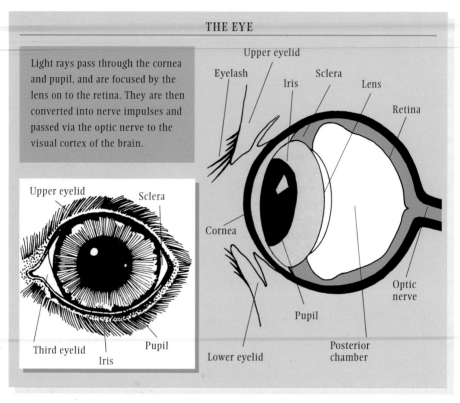

Cataract

This is an opacity of the lens in one or both eyes. The pupil appears greyish instead of the normal black colour. In advanced cases, the lens looks like a pearl and the dog may be blind. The many causes of cataract in Boxers include infection, diabetes mellitus and trauma.

URINARY SYSTEM DISEASES

Diseases producing increased thirst

■ Acute kidney failure
The most common infectious agent producing acute nephritis is leptospirosis (see Infectious diseases, page 105).

■ Chronic kidney failure
This is common in old dogs and occurs when persistent damage to the kidney results in toxic substances starting to accumulate in the blood stream.

Diseases causing blood in the urine

■ Cystitis
This is an infection of the bladder. It is more common in the bitch because the infection has easy access through the shorter urethra. The clinical signs include frequency of urination, straining and sometimes a bloody urine. In all other respects, the dog remains healthy.

THE URINARY SYSTEM

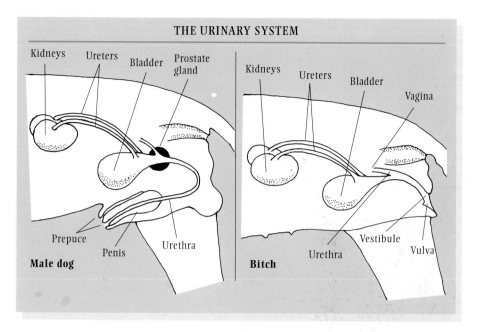

Kidneys Ureters Bladder Prostate gland Penis Prepuce Urethra **Male dog**

Kidneys Ureters Bladder Vagina Vestibule Vulva Urethra **Bitch**

■ **Urinary calculi or stones**
These can form in either the kidney or bladder.

■ **Kidney stones** can enter the ureters causing severe abdominal pain.

■ **Bladder stones,** or calculi, are fairly common in both sexes. In the bitch they are larger and straining is usually the only clinical sign. In the dog the most common sign is unproductive straining due to urinary obstruction.

■ **Tumours of the bladder**
These can occur and cause frequent straining and bloody urine, or, by occupying space within the bladder, cause incontinence.

Incontinence

This occasionally occurs for no apparent reason. Hormones or medicine to tighten the bladder sphincter can help.

REPRODUCTIVE ORGAN DISEASES

The male dog

■ **Retained testicle (cryptorchidism)**
Occasionally one or both testicles may fail to descend into the scrotum and remain somewhere along their developmental path. Surgery is advisable to remove retained testicles as they are very likely to develop cancer.

■ **Tumours**
These are fairly common but, fortunately, most are benign. One type of testicular tumour, known as a Sertoli cell tumour, produces female hormones leading to the development of female characteristics.

■ **Prostate disease**
This is common in the old dog. Usually a benign enlargement occurs where the prostate

THE REPRODUCTIVE SYSTEM

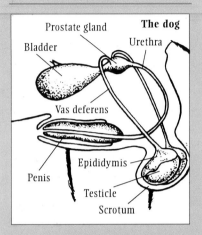

The dog

Prostate gland
Bladder
Urethra
Vas deferens
Epididymis
Penis
Testicle
Scrotum

Sperm and testosterone are produced in the male dog's testicles. Sperm pass into the epididymis for storage, thence via the vas deferens during mating.

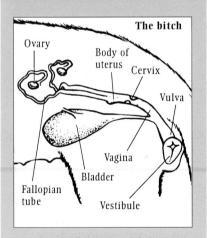

The bitch

Ovary
Body of uterus
Cervix
Vulva
Vagina
Bladder
Fallopian tube
Vestibule

Eggs are produced in the ovaries and enter the uterus through the fallopian tubes. During the heat period, they can be fertilized by sperm.

MAMMARY TUMOURS

These are common in the older entire bitch. Most are benign, but where malignant, they can grow rapidly and spread to other organs. Early surgical removal of any lump is advisable because of the danger of malignancy.

slowly increases in size. Hormone treatment or castration helps.

■ **Infection of the penis and sheath (balanitis)**
An increase and discolouration occurs in the discharge from the sheath, and the dog licks his penis more frequently.

■ **Paraphimosis**
Prolapse of the penis (see page 139).

■ **Castration**
This is of value in the treatment of behavioural problems. Excessive sexual activity, such as mounting cushions or other dogs, and territorial urination may be eliminated by castration, as may certain types of aggression and the desire to escape and wander off.

The bitch

■ **Pyometra**
This is a common and serious disease of the older bitch although bitches that have had puppies seem less likely to develop it. The treatment of choice for this condition is usually an ovariohysterectomy.

■ **Mastitis**
This is an infection of the mammary glands and occurs usually in lactating bitches. The affected glands become swollen, hard and painful (see Breeding, page 124).

FALSE (PSEUDO) PREGNANCY

This occurs in most bitches about eight to twelve weeks after oestrus at the stage when the bitch would be lactating had she been pregnant. The signs vary and include:
- Poor appetite
- Lethargy
- Milk production
- Nest building
- Aggressiveness
- Attachment to a substitute puppy which is often a squeaky toy

Note: Once a bitch has had a false pregnancy, she is likely to have one after each heat period.
- **Treatment,** if needed, is by hormones, and prevention is by a hormone injection, or tablets, and long-term by an ovariohysterectomy.

Birth control

- **Hormone therapy**
Several preparations, injections and tablets are available to prevent or postpone the bitch's heat period.
- **Spaying (ovariohysterectomy)**
This is an operation to remove the uterus and ovaries, usually performed when the bitch is not on heat.

NERVOUS SYSTEM DISEASES

The nervous system consists of two parts:
1 The central nervous system (CNS) consists of the brain and the spinal cord which runs in the vertebral column.

2 The peripheral nervous system includes all the nerves that connect the CNS to the organs of the body.
- **Canine distemper virus**
(See Infectious diseases, page 105.)
- **Vestibular syndrome**
This is a fairly common condition of the older dog, and affects that part of the brain that controls balance. There is a sudden head tilt to the affected side, often flicking movements of the eyes called nystagmus, and the dog may fall or circle to that side. Many dogs will recover slowly but the condition may recur.
- **Slug bait (Metaldehyde) poisoning**
The dog appears 'drunk', uncoordinated, and may have convulsions. There is no specific treatment, but sedation will often lead to recovery in a large dog like the Boxer.
- **Epilepsy**
This is a nervous disorder that is seen occasionally in the Boxer.
Treatment: this is by the use of anti-convulsant drugs.
- **Progressive axonopathy**
This is a degenerative disease of the peripheral nerves. It is an inherited disease of the Boxer. There is no treatment available.

BONE, MUSCLE AND JOINT DISEASES

Note: X-rays are necessary to confirm any diagnosis involving bone.

- **Bone infection (osteomyelitis)**
This usually occurs after an injury such as a bite, or where a broken bone protrudes through the skin. Signs are pain, heat and swelling over the site, and if a limb bone is affected, there can be severe lameness.

■ **Fractures**

Any break or crack in a bone is called a fracture. When a vet repairs a fracture, his aim is to replace the fractured ends of bone into their normal position and then to immobilize the bone for four to six weeks. Depending on the bone, and type of fracture, there are several methods available – cage rest, external casts, or surgery to perform internal fixation, e.g. by plating or pinning.

■ **Bone tumours**

These are not common, except in the giant breeds, but they are known to occur in the Boxer. The most common sites are the radius, humerus and femur. Bone tumours are very painful, and they tend to be malignant and spread to other parts of the body early in the course of the disease. Amputation of the limb will remove the primary tumour but as it may have already spread to other areas, it is often not feasible. Radiotherapy and chemotherapy are not normally successful.

■ **A sprain**

This is an inflammation of an over-stretched joint. The joint is hot, swollen, and painful, and the dog is lame.

■ **Cruciate ligament rupture**

When these rupture, as a result of a severe sprain, the stifle or knee joint is destabilized and the dog becomes instantly and severely lame on that leg. This usually occurs in middle-aged, overweight dogs. Surgical repair is usually necessary.

■ **Arthritis or degenerative joint disease**

This is fairly common in the older Boxer. It

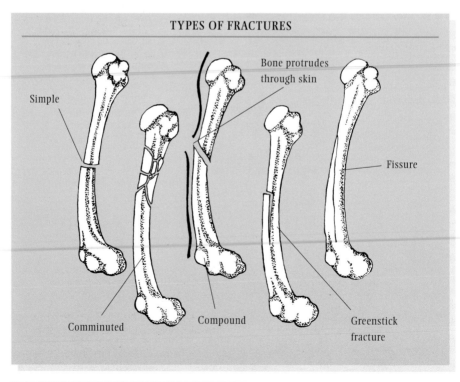

TYPES OF FRACTURES

Simple

Bone protrudes through skin

Fissure

Comminuted

Compound

Greenstick fracture

THE SKELETON

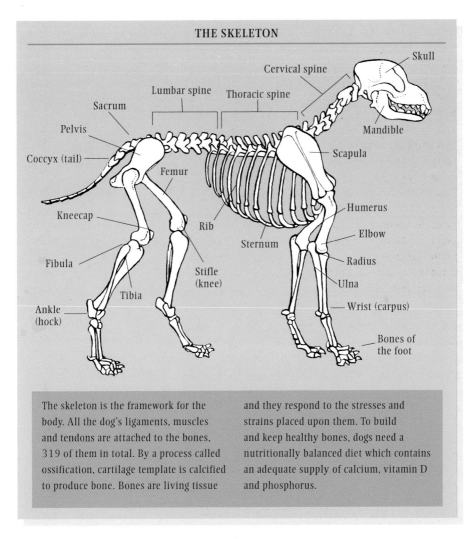

Skull
Cervical spine
Lumbar spine
Thoracic spine
Sacrum
Pelvis
Coccyx (tail)
Femur
Mandible
Scapula
Kneecap
Rib
Humerus
Sternum
Elbow
Fibula
Stifle (knee)
Radius
Ulna
Tibia
Ankle (hock)
Wrist (carpus)
Bones of the foot

The skeleton is the framework for the body. All the dog's ligaments, muscles and tendons are attached to the bones, 319 of them in total. By a process called ossification, cartilage template is calcified to produce bone. Bones are living tissue and they respond to the stresses and strains placed upon them. To build and keep healthy bones, dogs need a nutritionally balanced diet which contains an adequate supply of calcium, vitamin D and phosphorus.

results in thickening of the joint capsule, formation of abnormal new bone around the edges of the joint and, sometimes, wearing of the joint cartilage. The joint becomes enlarged and painful, and has a reduced range of movement. It tends to occur in the older dog and is usually a problem of the hips, stifles and elbows.

■ **Spondylitis**

This is arthritis of the spine. It is also common in the older Boxer and causes weakness and stiffness of the hindquarters (see Special problems of the Boxer, page 103).

CHAPTER EIGHT

BREEDING

If properly planned, breeding a litter from your own dog or bitch can be rewarding and great fun. The secret of successful breeding is to use good stock, to plan ahead so you have plenty of time, to understand that you could be unsuccessful, and to be aware in advance of the needs of the bitch and puppies. Boxers can have large litters — seven or more puppies are not unusual — so you do need to make sure you can find good homes for this number.

Action prior to mating

1 Locate the right dog of the opposite sex. This will be of good and known temperament, and should be free of inherited or contagious disease. Hyperplastic gingivitis, spondylitis, progressive axonopathy and cardiomyopathy are four inherited defects that you should ensure are not carried in either dog's line.

■ The temperament of both parents is all important. Remember that the puppies will almost certainly be going to caring family homes, and with a lively, active breed like the Boxer, it is essential that they end up well balanced, calm, sociable individuals.

2 Check both pedigrees (family trees) to ensure that you are not breeding from a dog and bitch who are too closely related.

3 If possible, allow the dogs to get to know each other before mating.

MATING

A Boxer bitch should not be mated until she matures, usually at one-and-a-half to two years old, and the male would normally be at least that age. The bitch comes into heat on average twice a year, for about three weeks at a time. The vulva swells, and bleeding starts; initially fairly runny, this becomes darker and more tacky as she approaches ovulation. This fertile time is usually ten to twelve days after the heat started.

When she is ready to accept the male, the bitch will stand with her tail raised to one side. The male mounts the bitch and the penis is usually locked into position inside the female, producing the so-called 'tie'. After a minute or so, the male lifts one hind leg over her back and places it on the ground. The two dogs stand back to back for up to twenty minutes until the penis subsides and they can separate. This tie ensures that the maximum amount of sperm reaches the uterus and increases the chances of fertilization. A tie is not essential and pregnancies frequently result from 'slip' services where ejaculation occurs without a tie.

■ With a novice bitch it may be necessary to hold her gently while she is mated to reassure her. It is advisable to mate the two dogs at least twice on successive days, but a greater success rate is achieved if the dogs are allowed to run together on several successive days.

Mismating

If an unwanted mating has occurred your vet can give the bitch a hormone injection to prevent fertilization. This must be given within three days of the mating.

120

Bitch will not mate

■ The stage of heat may not be correct. If in doubt, your vet can take blood samples or vaginal swabs to ascertain whether she is at the correct stage to mate.

■ Failure to complete the mating may be due to a stricture within the vagina, or the bitch may have unrelated problems, such as hip pain. If she shows signs of discomfort and moves away, consult your vet.

No pregnancy

Try again at the next heat and consider a

different male. There may be nothing wrong individually with either the dog or bitch but together they may be incompatible.

Paraphimosis

This is a prolonged erection of the penis which is unable to retract back into the sheath after mating. It becomes very swollen due to constriction by the sheath. The exposed penis should be bathed in cool sterile water to reduce it in size, and lubrication with petroleum jelly or soap should make it possible to pull the sheath forward over the penis. If correction proves impossible, veterinary help is needed.

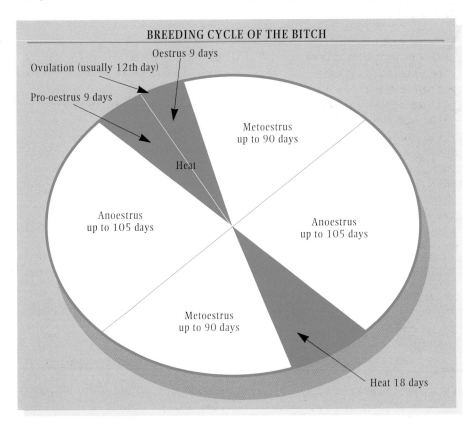

BREEDING CYCLE OF THE BITCH

Oestrus 9 days

Ovulation (usually 12th day)

Pro-oestrus 9 days

Metoestrus up to 90 days

Heat

Anoestrus up to 105 days

Anoestrus up to 105 days

Metoestrus up to 90 days

Heat 18 days

PREGNANCY

Pregnancy is normally sixty-three days. For the first three weeks, there is little change in the bitch. She may be quieter than normal and look plump. The teats and breasts may begin to enlarge.

■ About four weeks after mating, your vet may be able to detect pregnancy by feeling her abdomen. There is also a blood test that can detect pregnancy at this stage. Ultrasound examination is now available in an increasing number of veterinary practices, and this can be used to detect pregnancy after twenty-eight days.

■ At about six weeks, the bitch's abdomen begins to increase in size, and the teats and mammary glands begin to enlarge — in a Boxer, there may be considerable enlargement of the teats. She may become quieter but her appetite remains good. Food intake should be increased and she should be on a balanced, calcium-rich diet. There are excellent commercial complete diets available for this purpose. Ideally, a 'growth-formula' diet should be introduced at the sixth week of pregnancy, and continued throughout pregnancy and lactation, so that the bitch and puppies are on the same diet from late pregnancy onwards. About a week before she is due to give birth (whelp), milk may start to ooze from the teats.

BIRTH

A whelping box should be prepared in advance. There will be a lot of discharge during the birth and it is a good idea to line the box with several layers of newspaper which can gradually be removed as they become soiled. The bitch should be able to stretch out in either direction with the safety bar in place. An infra-red heat source positioned directly over the whelping area is essential to prevent hypothermia developing in the puppies, because they are unable to regulate their own body temperature until they are about ten to fourteen days old. The whelping room should be warm and quiet, and supervision of the whelping should be by someone the bitch knows and trusts.

■ Labour starts gradually, the bitch just appearing restless. She usually bed-makes by tearing up newspaper or scattering blankets around. This initial stage can last for up to twenty-four hours but it is usually much shorter. The bitch's temperature will drop from 38.5°C (101.5°F) to about 36°C (97°F), and towards the end of this period the contractions begin.

■ These contractions gradually increase in frequency until she is contracting several times each minute, and a water bag appears at the vulva. A puppy is usually born within twenty minutes of the onset of regular rhythmical contractions, but this can take up to two hours in a normal whelping. From this stage the interval between puppies varies enormously, even up to twelve hours.

THE PLACENTA

If the placenta (afterbirth) is passed, it will usually be eaten by the bitch. This should be encouraged. It may, however, become detached and remain inside the uterus, slowly disintegrating and being expelled from the uterus as a darkish discharge over the next few weeks. This is perfectly normal.

However, an interval of ten to sixty minutes between each puppy is more likely.

- The bitch will usually lick the puppy immediately on birth. This ruptures the bag and revives the puppy who will begin to cry as he fills his lungs for the first time. If the bitch ignores the puppy or seems confused, you must gently tear the membranes from around it, hold it in a towel, wipe out the mouth and vigorously rub the puppy to stimulate breathing. If the placenta is still attached to the puppy, the umbilical cord should be tied with cotton about 4 cm (1^1/$_2$ in) from the puppy and then carefully cut with scissors on the side of the knot away from the puppy, who should be placed gently onto a teat to begin suckling. Do not pull on the umbilical cord as this can lead to an umbilical hernia in the puppy.

The bitch will pay some attention to each puppy when it is born but will not be very interested in the litter until whelping is

WHELPING PROBLEMS

- **Primary inertia**

The bitch fails to start contracting. If whelping does not follow within twenty-four hours of the onset of signs of restlessness, if the bitch is more than one day overdue, or if a green vaginal discharge is noticed, she should be examined by a vet. This is not common in a vigorous breed like a Boxer.

- **Secondary inertia**

This usually follows a prolonged unproductive labour where, due to an obstruction called a dystocia, birth cannot take place and the bitch becomes exhausted. This can be caused by an abnormally positioned or sized foetus (foetal dystocia), or by a uterine obstruction (maternal dystocia). An obstructing puppy may be manually removed by the vet or a Caesarean section may be necessary.

- **Dystocia**

This is suspected where the bitch has been contracting unproductively for over two hours. In this case the vet must always be called. Possible causes include:

- A previous pelvic fracture which has caused a narrowing of the birth canal.
- A twisted uterus.
- An overlarge puppy or, in Boxers, an overlarge head.
- A congenitally abnormal puppy.
- A malpresentation.

- **Presentation**

Puppies are normally born either head and forelegs first (anterior presentation) or tail and back legs first (posterior presentation). Any variation on this is called a malpresentation and can cause foetal dystocia. Two common examples are:

- **Breech presentation** — the tail of the puppy is coming first but the hind legs are tucked up forwards under the puppy's abdomen. This enlarges the buttocks of the puppy and thereby causes an obstruction.
- **Head first with forelegs pointing backwards** — delivery is prevented because the shoulder area is enlarged.

Note: all these obstructions will require veterinary attention and assisted birth, or a Caesarean section may be necessary.

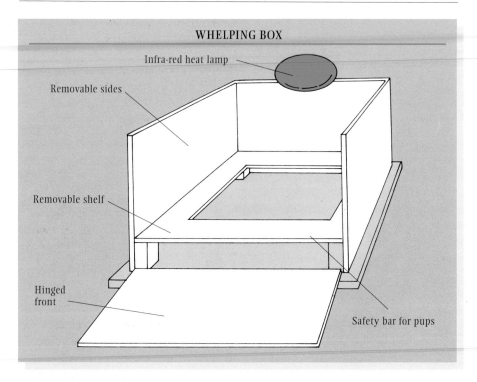

WHELPING BOX

Infra-red heat lamp

Removable sides

Removable shelf

Hinged front

Safety bar for pups

complete, when a change in her attitude is obvious. She will brighten up, clean herself thoroughly and begin to look after the puppies in earnest.

POSTNATAL CARE

The bitch

■ **Feeding**
During this lactation phase, the pups are making maximum demands on the bitch, and it is essential that she is fed a fully nutritious diet. Simply supplementing with calcium is not enough. The best diet is a quality complete-growth diet formulated for the lactating bitch, and she should be fed almost on demand.

Possible problems

■ **Vaginal discharge** — a greenish brown discharge is normal for the first few days and may continue for several weeks.

■ **Post-whelping metritis** — this is very serious. The bitch is very ill with a raised temperature, and has a profuse foul vaginal discharge. A vet should always be consulted without delay.

■ **No milk** — the puppies fail to thrive and cry continuously. It is essential to supplement feeding with a foster feeding bottle and synthetic milk available from your vet.

■ **Mastitis** — this can occur in over-engorged mammary glands. Check daily that no breasts are sore, very hard or hot.

■ **Behavioural change** — the bitch may

EXERCISE

During the first few days the bitch will not want to be away from the pups for long and will not require exercise to any degree. She will, of course, require frequent access to the outside for toileting purposes, and may appreciate a short walk for a change of scene. She may or may not want your company.

become very protective of her puppies and be aggressive to her owners. She should be left alone to start with, but the pups must be checked regularly in her absence. After a few days, her worries usually subside and she becomes trusting again. If handling is necessary, for instance to supplement the pups, a muzzle may be necessary.

■ **Aggression to puppies** — this can occur initially, and the bitch must be muzzled or separated from the pups. Usually this is caused by fright or confusion, or is due to displaced excessive cleaning. Hold the puppies on to her forcibly to be suckled for a while, and she will normally accept them.

■ **Eclampsia** — this is a very serious condition and can be fatal. The blood calcium level of the bitch becomes too low due to the demands of the pups on her milk and she begins to show nervous symptoms. Initially she starts to twitch or shiver and appears unsteady. This rapidly progresses to staggering, then convulsions. The vet must be contacted immediately as an injection of calcium is essential to save the life of the bitch.

The pups should be partially or completely weaned to ensure the eclampsia does not recur. The time of onset varies but it is usually seen

when the pups are about three weeks old and making maximum demands on her. With large litters, supplementing the puppies' feeding to relieve the load on the dam would seem to be a logical approach to prevention, although other factors can be involved.

■ **Squashed puppy** — this accident can be prevented by the correct whelping box design.

The puppies

Hypothermia is the commonest cause of death in unweaned puppies. The whelping area or box must be kept warm by a direct heat source such as an infra-red lamp or an electric blanket. A warm room is not usually sufficient.

Days one and two

■ Check for any obvious congenital abnormalities, such as hare lip, cleft palate, and undershot or overshot jaws. In Boxers, some degree of undershot jaw is normal and desirable. If in doubt the vet should be asked to attend.

WORMING

Roundworm larvae are passed to the puppies while still in the uterus via the placenta, and after birth through the milk. This can be minimized by giving a larvicidal wormer to the bitch during pregnancy and lactation. Your vet should be consulted for details of dose and timing. In addition, the bitch should be dosed each time the puppies are wormed to prevent the build-up of a roundworm burden within the litter and its environment.

PET HEALTH INSURANCE AND VETS' FEES

Pet health insurance and vets' fees By choosing your dog wisely and then ensuring that he is fit, the right weight, occupied both mentally and physically, protected against disease by vaccination, and fed correctly, you should be able to minimize any vet's bills. The unexpected may well happen though. Accidents and injuries do occur, and dogs can develop life-long allergies or long-term illnesses such as diabetes. Pet health insurance is available and is recommended by the vast majority of veterinarians for such unexpected eventualities. It is important to take out a policy that will suit you and your Boxer, so it is always wise to ask your veterinary surgeon for his recommendation.

■ Ensure that the puppies all suckle the bitch on the first day. This is important as her first milk (colostrum) is rich in antibodies and enables them to withstand infections during their first six to twelve weeks of life.
■ Ensure that the puppies are having enough to drink. A quiet litter is usually a happy, well-fed litter. If any puppies are weaker, it may be necessary to supplement them with synthetic bitch's milk using a foster feeder bottle.

Days three to five

■ If dew claws are present on the hind legs, they should be removed as they protrude and often tear and bleed when the dog is older. Boxers commonly have their front dew claws removed although it is certainly not essential.

This is carried out at three to five days of age.
■ Tail docking has been customary in this breed, but in the UK it is now illegal for anyone except a veterinary surgeon to perform this. If a vet decides that it is in the puppy's interest to do this, it will be done at three to five days of age and the tail will usually be shortened to about 1 cm ($1/2$ in).

Days five to fourteen

■ Fading puppy syndrome is when puppies fade and die for no apparent reason. It is essential that the vet is consulted. A dead puppy is useful for a post mortem examination. The cause may be hypothermia, infection, lack of food, lack of colostrum, trauma from the bitch, roundworms or any stress.
■ The eyes open at ten to fourteen days, and abnormalities can be noticed now. An eye may be absent, or smaller than normal. These are both congenital abnormalities, but are not common in the Boxer.
■ Treat for roundworms at fourteen days; consult your vet for advice on this.

Days fourteen to twenty-one

■ The pups become more mobile and at three weeks are quite lively and capable of wandering out of the whelping area. This is a useful period to begin socializing them by frequent handling and exposure to household events and noises. The bed should be moved from time to time to create an environmental challenge for the puppies.

Days twenty-one to forty-two

■ At twenty-one days weaning can begin. The pups should be taught to lap proprietary or skimmed cow's milk initially. Soon they can be tried with porridge-style cereals, scraped fish or finely minced chicken. Feed them several times a day but at this stage they will also be suckling the bitch.

■ By twenty-eight days they should have progressed on to four or five small meals a day, preferably of a good-quality commercial complete puppy-growth formula food. Alternatively, meat (fresh or canned puppy food) with, say, soaked human or puppy cereals can be given. A balanced vitamin and mineral supplement should only be added to home-prepared food as growth-formula food for puppies contains the right balance.

■ At twenty-eight days the puppies should be wormed again, and then at intervals of two weeks up to the age of three months, using a safe, effective veterinary wormer. Thereafter worming should be carried out monthly until six months of age, and then two to four times a year for the rest of their lives.

■ The pups should be handled gently but often by all family members, and should be exposed to all household noises. Their environment should be quite challenging, and rich in toys, cardboard boxes, balls and other interesting playthings.

NEW HOMES

The best age for a Boxer puppy to adapt to a new family is when he is between six and eight weeks of age, so this is the age at which you should aim to sell the pups. Remember that the puppy will make a better pet if you and your family have been gently playing with him and handling him. Before parting with a puppy you should:

■ Interview the prospective purchasers to ensure that they will give him a caring home and that a Boxer will suit their life-style.

■ Ensure that he is fit and well.

■ Prepare a diet sheet to give to the new owners.

■ Ask your vet whether the puppies should have their first vaccination. If this is done, hand out the vaccination certificate and tell the new owners when the next one is due.

■ Inform the new owners when the puppy was wormed, with what, and when the next dose is due.

■ Prepare the pedigree form, and hand it over to the new owners.

■ Take out a temporary pet health insurance policy on the puppy. This lasts for six weeks and the new owner should be advised to continue it. It relieves you of the worry of any unforeseen illness or problem in the first few weeks after purchase. It is not expensive and your vet will give you details. Registration of puppies with the Kennel Club now carries free pet insurance for the first six weeks. Other schemes exist whereby your vet can issue the new owner with a free month's instant pet insurance cover at the time of vaccination.

■ And, above all, emphasise the need for early socialization with people, dogs, cats and other animals, such as sheep, and early exposure to normal household noises such as washing machines, vacuum cleaners, radios and television.

CHAPTER NINE

FIRST AID, ACCIDENTS AND EMERGENCIES

First aid is the emergency care given to a dog suffering injury or illness of sudden onset.

AIMS OF FIRST AID

1 Keep the dog alive.
2 Prevent unnecessary suffering.
3 Prevent further injury.

RULES OF FIRST AID

Keep calm. If you panic you will be unable to help effectively.

Contact a vet as soon as possible. Advice given over the telephone may be life-saving.

Avoid injury to yourself. A distressed or injured animal may bite so use a muzzle if necessary (see muzzling, page 139).

Control haemorrhage. Excessive blood loss can lead to severe shock and death (see haemorrhage, page 132).

5

Maintain an airway. Failure to breathe or obtain adequate oxygen can lead to brain damage or loss of life within five minutes (see airway obstruction and artificial respiration, page 130).

COMMON ACCIDENTS AND EMERGENCIES

The following common accidents and emergencies all require first aid action. In an emergency, your priorities are to keep the dog alive and comfortable until he can be examined by a vet. In many cases, there is effective action that you can take immediately to help preserve your dog's health and life.

SHOCK AND ROAD ACCIDENTS

SHOCK

This is a serious clinical syndrome which can cause death. Shock can follow road accidents, severe burns, electrocution, extremes of heat and cold, heart failure, poisoning, severe fluid loss, reactions to drugs, insect stings or snake bite.

SIGNS OF SHOCK

- Weakness or collapse
- Pale gums
- Cold extremities, e.g. feet and ears
- Weak pulse and rapid heart
- Rapid, shallow breathing

RECOMMENDED ACTION

1 Act immediately. Give cardiac massage (see page 131) and/or artificial respiration (see page 131) if necessary, after checking for a clear airway.

2 Keep the dog flat and warm. Control external haemorrhage (page 132).

3 Veterinary treatment is essential thereafter.

ROAD ACCIDENTS

Injuries resulting from a fast-moving vehicle colliding with an animal can be very serious. Road accidents may result in:

- Death
- Head injuries
- Spinal damage
- Internal haemorrhage, bruising and rupture of major organs, e.g. liver, spleen, kidneys
- Fractured ribs and lung damage, possibly resulting in haemothorax (blood in the chest cavity) or pneumothorax (air in the chest cavity)
- Fractured limbs with or without nerve damage
- External haemorrhage, wounds, tears and bruising

RECOMMENDED ACTION

1 Assess the situation and move the dog to a safe position. Use a blanket to transport him and keep him flat.

2 Check for signs of life: feel for a heart beat (see cardiac massage, page 131), and watch for the rise and fall of the chest wall.

3 If the dog is breathing, treat as for shock (see above). If he is not breathing but there is a heart beat, give artificial respiration, after checking for airway obstruction. Consider the use of a muzzle (see muzzling, page 139).

4 Control external haemorrhage (see haemorrhage, page 132).

5 Keep the dog warm and flat at all times, and seek veterinary help.

AIRWAY OBSTRUCTION

■ **FOREIGN BODY IN THE THROAT,** e.g. a ball.

RECOMMENDED ACTION

1

This is an acute emergency. Do not try to pull out the object. Push it upwards and forwards from behind the throat so that it moves from its position, where it is obstructing the larynx, into the mouth.

2

The dog should now be able to breathe. Remove the object from his mouth.

DROWNING

RECOMMENDED ACTION

1

Out of the water, remove collar and place dog on his side with his head lower than his body.

2

With hands, apply firm downward pressure on chest at five-second intervals.

■ **FOLLOWING A ROAD ACCIDENT,** or convulsion, blood, saliva or vomit in the throat may obstruct breathing.

■ The Boxer, in common with other very short-nosed (brachycephalic) breeds, suffers a higher risk of airway obstruction due to the fact that the nasal cavity may be narrow and the soft palate is often relatively long. An over-long soft palate can further compromise breathing in cases of physical airway obstruction, and can block the entrance to the upper airway (larynx).

RECOMMENDED ACTION

Pull the tongue forwards and clear any obstruction with your fingers. Then, with the dog on his side, extend the head and neck forward to maintain a clear airway.

RECOMMENDED ACTION

1	**2**
Pull the tongue forwards and clear any obstruction with your fingers.	Then, with the dog on his side, extend the head and neck forwards to maintain a clear airway.

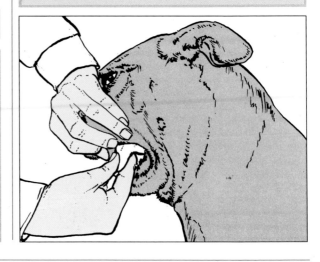

130

ARTIFICIAL RESPIRATION

The method for helping a dog which has a clear airway but cannot breathe.

RECOMMENDED ACTION

Use mouth-to-mouth resuscitation by cupping your hands over his nose and mouth and blowing into his nostrils every five seconds.

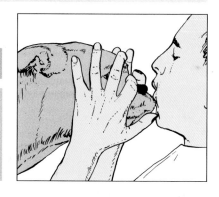

CARDIAC MASSAGE

This is required if your dog's heart fails.

RECOMMENDED ACTION

With the dog lying on his right side, feel for a heart beat with your fingers on the chest wall behind the dog's elbows on his left side.

If you feel nothing, squeeze rhythmically with your palms, placing one hand on top of the other, as shown, at two-second intervals, pressing down hard.

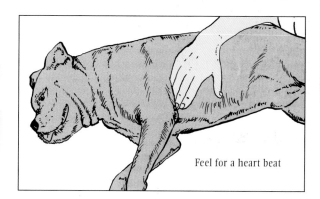

Feel for a heart beat

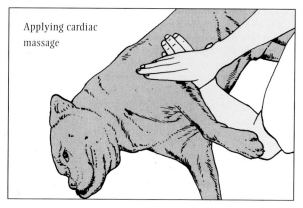

Applying cardiac massage

131

HAEMORRHAGE

Severe haemorrhage must be controlled, as it leads to a precipitous fall in blood pressure and the onset of shock. Haemorrhage is likely to result from deep surface wounds, or internal injuries, e.g. following a road accident.

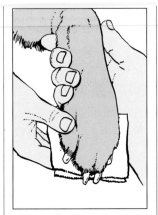

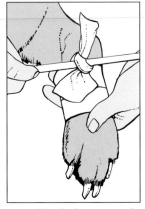

■ **FOR SURFACE WOUNDS**

RECOMMENDED ACTION

Locate the bleeding point and apply pressure either with:
■ **Your thumb** or
■ **A pressure bandage** (preferred method) or
■ **A tourniquet**

1 **Pressure bandage**
Use a pad of gauze, cotton wool or cloth against the wound and tightly bandage around it. In the absence of a proper dressing, use a clean handkerchief or scarf.

2 If the bleeding continues, apply another dressing on top of the first.

1 **Tourniquet**
(on limbs and tail)
Tie a narrow piece of cloth, a neck tie or dog lead tightly around the limb, nearer to the body than the wound itself.

2 Using a pencil or stick within the knot, twist until it becomes tight enough to stop the blood flow.

3 **Important**: you must seek veterinary assistance as soon as possible.

Note: Tourniquets should be applied for no longer than fifteen minutes at a time, or tissue death may result.

■ **FOR INTERNAL BLEEDING**

RECOMMENDED ACTION

1 You should keep the animal quiet and warm, and minimize any movement.

2 **Important**: you must seek veterinary assistance as soon as possible.

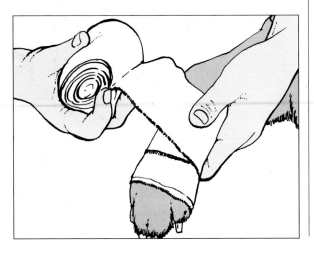

WOUNDS

These may result from road accidents, dog fights, sharp stones or glass, etc. Deep wounds may cause serious bleeding, bone or nerve damage.

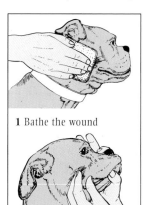

1 Bathe the wound

2 Apply antiseptic cream

RECOMMENDED ACTION

1 Deal with external bleeding (see haemorrhage, opposite) and keep the dog quiet before seeking veterinary attention.

2 Cut feet or pads should be bandaged to prevent further blood loss.

3 Minor cuts, abrasions and bruising should be bathed with warm salt solution (one 5ml teaspoonful per 550ml (1 pint) of water). They should be protected from further injury or contamination. Apply some antiseptic cream, if necessary.

4 If in doubt, ask your vet in case a wound needs suturing or antibiotic therapy is needed, particularly if caused by fighting. Even minor cuts and punctures can be complicated by the presence of a foreign body.

FRACTURES

Broken bones, especially in the legs, often result from road accidents. Be careful when lifting and transporting the affected dog.

■ **LEG FRACTURES**

RECOMMENDED ACTION

1 Broken lower leg bones can sometimes be straightened gently, bandaged and then taped or tied with string to a make-shift splint, e.g. a piece of wood or rolled-up newspaper or cardboard.

2 Otherwise, support the leg to prevent any movement. Take the dog to the vet immediately.

■ **OTHER FRACTURES**
These may be more difficult to diagnose. If you suspect a fracture, transport your dog very gently with great care, and get him to the vet.

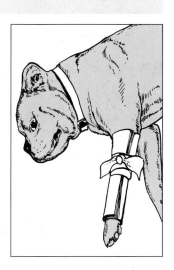

OTHER ACCIDENTS AND EMERGENCIES

OTHER ACCIDENTS AND EMERGENCIES

COLLAPSE

This may be accompanied by loss of consciousness, but not in every case.

POSSIBLE CAUSES

- Head trauma, e.g. following a road accident
- Heart failure
- Stroke
- Hyperthermia (heat-stroke)
- Hypothermia (cold)
- Hypocalcaemia (low calcium)
- Shock
- Spinal fractures
- Asphyxia (interference with breathing)
- Electrocution
- Poisoning
- Tracheal collapse

Note: you should refer to the relevant section for further details of these problems.

- Boxers are considered to be be more prone to collapse or 'fainting' due to upper airway or cardiac problems in some individuals.

RECOMMENDED ACTION

1 The collapsed animal must be moved with care to avoid causing any further damage.

2 Gently slide him on his side onto a blanket or a coat.

3 Check he is breathing, and then keep him quiet and warm until you obtain professional help from a vet.

4 If he is not breathing, you must administer artificial respiration immediately, after checking that the dog has a clear airway (see page 130).

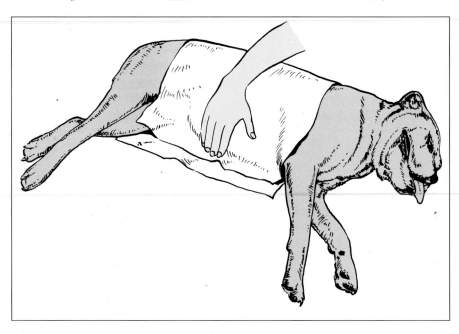

CONVULSIONS (FITS OR SEIZURES)

These are very alarming to dog owners. Uncontrolled spasms, 'paddling' of legs, loss of consciousness, sometimes salivation and involuntary urination or defecation occur. Most convulsions only last a few minutes, but the dog is often confused and dazed afterwards.

POSSIBLE CAUSES

- Poisoning
- Head injuries
- Brain tumours
- Liver and kidney disease
- Meningitis
- Epilepsy
- Low blood glucose, e.g. in diabetes, or low blood calcium, e.g. in eclampsia

RECOMMENDED ACTION

1 Unless he is in a dangerous situation, do not attempt to hold the dog, but protect him from damaging himself.

2 Do not give him anything by mouth.

3 Try to keep him quiet, cool and in a darkened room until he sees the vet.

4 If you have to move him, cover him with a blanket first.

HEART FAILURE

This is not as common as in humans, but commoner in Boxers than most breeds. Affected dogs faint, usually during exercise, and lose consciousness. The mucous membranes appear pale or slightly blue. (See heart and circulation diseases, pages 106-107, and Special problems of the Boxer, page 103.)

RECOMMENDED ACTION

1 Cover the dog in a blanket, and then lie him on his side.

2 Massage the dog's chest behind the elbows (see cardiac massage, page 131).

3 When he recovers, take the dog straight to the vet.

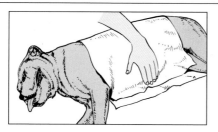
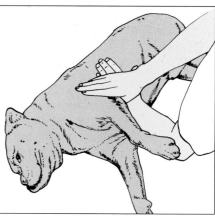

1 An affected dog should be covered with a blanket and laid on his side.
2 Apply cardiac massage, pressing down firmly at two-second intervals.

HEAT-STROKE

This occurs in hot weather, especially when dogs have been left in cars with insufficient ventilation. Affected animals are extremely distressed, panting and possibly collapsed. They can die rapidly. A heat-stroke case should be treated as an acute emergency. The narrow nostrils and nasal cavity of the Boxer render this breed more susceptible to heat stress because deep inspiration through the nose is difficult.

RECOMMENDED ACTION

1 Place the dog in a cold bath or run cold water over his body until his temperature is in the normal range.

2 Offer water with added salt (one 5ml teaspoonful per half litre/ 18 fl oz water).

3 Treatment for shock may be necessary (see page 129).

ELECTROCUTION

This is most likely to occur in a bored puppy who chews through a cable. Electrocution may kill him outright or lead to delayed shock.

■ **DO NOT TOUCH HIM BEFORE YOU SWITCH OFF THE ELECTRICITY SOURCE.**

RECOMMENDED ACTION

1 If he is not breathing, begin artificial respiration immediately (see page 130) and keep him warm.

2 Contact your vet; if he survives he will need treatment for shock (see page 129).

BURNS AND SCALDS

POSSIBLE CAUSES
■ Spilled hot drinks, boiling water or fat.
■ Friction, chemical and electrical burns.

RECOMMENDED ACTION

1 Immediately apply running cold water and, thereafter, cold compresses, ice packs or packets of frozen peas to the affected area.

2 Veterinary attention is essential in most cases.

SNAKE BITE

This is due to the adder in Great Britain. Signs are pain accompanied by a soft swelling around two puncture wounds, usually on either the head, neck or limbs. Trembling, collapse, shock and even death can ensue.

RECOMMENDED ACTION

1 Do not let the dog walk; carry him to the car.

2 Keep him warm, and take him immediately to the vet.

FOREIGN BODIES

■ **IN THE MOUTH**
Sticks or bones wedged between the teeth cause frantic pawing at the mouth and salivation.

RECOMMENDED ACTION

Remove the foreign body with your fingers or pliers. Use a wooden block placed between the dog's canine teeth if possible to aid the safety of this procedure. Some objects have to be removed under general anaesthesia.
Note: a ball in the throat is dealt with in airway obstruction (see page 130), and is a critical emergency.

■ **FISH HOOKS**
Never try to pull these out, wherever they are.

RECOMMENDED ACTION

Cut the end of the fish hook with pliers and then push the barbed end through the skin and out.

■ **IN THE FOOT**
Glass, thorns or splinters can penetrate the pads or soft skin, causing pain, and infection if neglected.

RECOMMENDED ACTION

Soak the foot in warm salt

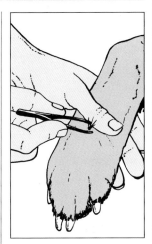

water and then use a sharp sterilized needle or pair of tweezers to extract the foreign body. If this is not possible, take your dog to the vet who will remove it under local or general anaesthetic if necessary.

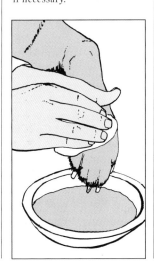

NOSE BLEEDS

These may be caused by trauma or violent sneezing, but are also related in some cases to ulceration of the lining of the nasal cavity.

RECOMMENDED ACTION

1 Keep the dog quiet and use ice packs on the nose.

2 Contact your vet if the bleeding persists.

EYEBALL PROLAPSE

This is not a common problem in Boxers, but it may arise from head trauma, e.g. following a dog fight. The eye is forced out of its socket and sight is lost unless it is replaced within fifteen minutes.

RECOMMENDED ACTION

1 Speed is essential. One person should pull the eyelids apart while the other gently presses the eyeball back into its socket, using moist sterile gauze or cloth.

2 If this is impossible, cover the eye with moist sterile gauze and take him to your vet immediately.

OTHER ACCIDENTS AND EMERGENCIES

GASTRIC DILATION

This is an emergency and cannot be treated at home. The stomach distends with gas and froth which the dog cannot easily eliminate. In some cases, the stomach then rotates and a torsion occurs, so the gases cannot escape at all and the stomach rapidly fills the abdomen. This causes pain, respiratory distress and circulatory failure. Life-threatening shock follows.

PREVENTIVE ACTION

1 Avoid the problem by not exercising your dog vigorously for two hours after a full meal.

2 If your dog is becoming bloated and has difficulty breathing, he is unlikely to survive unless he has veterinary attention within half an hour of the onset of symptoms, so get him to the vet immediately.

POISONING

Dogs can be poisoned by pesticides, herbicides, poisonous plants, paints, antifreeze or an overdose of drugs (animal or human).

■ If poisoning is suspected, first try to determine the agent involved, and find out if it is corrosive or not. This may be indicated on the container, but may also be evident from the blistering of the lips, gums and tongue, and increased salivation.

RECOMMENDED ACTION

■ **CORROSIVE POISONS**

1 Wash the inside of the dog's mouth.

2 Give him milk and bread to protect the gut against the effects of the corrosive.

3 Seek veterinary help.

■ **OTHER POISONS**

1 If the dog is conscious, make him vomit within half an hour of taking the poison.

2 A crystal of washing soda or a few 15ml tablespoonfuls of strong salt solution can be given carefully by mouth.

3 Retain a sample of vomit to aid identification of the poison, or take the poison container with you to show the vet. There may be a specific antidote, and any information can help in treatment.

STINGS

Bee and wasp stings often occur around the head, front limbs or mouth. The dog usually shows sudden pain and paws at, or licks, the stung area. A soft, painful swelling appears; sometimes the dog seems unwell or lethargic. Stings in the mouth and throat can be distressing and dangerous. In Boxers, it is also more prevalent for stings to cause an acute skin reaction (see Urticaria, page 111).

RECOMMENDED ACTION

1 Withdraw the sting (bees).

2 Then you can bathe the area in:
■ Vinegar for wasps
■ Bicarbonate for bees

3 An antihistamine injection may be needed. Take your dog to the vet and ask him for advice.

BREEDING

ECLAMPSIA

(See breeding, page 125)
This emergency may occur in your Boxer bitch when suckling her puppies, usually when they are about three weeks old.

PARAPHIMOSIS

(See breeding, page 121)
This problem may occur after mating, in the male. The engorged penis is unable to retract into the sheath.

MUZZLING

This will allow a nervous, distressed or injured dog to be examined safely, without the risk of being bitten. A tape or bandage is secured around the muzzle as illustrated. However, a muzzle should not be applied in the following circumstances:

■ Airway obstruction
■ Loss of consciousness
■ Compromised breathing or severe chest injury

1 Tie a knot in the bandage.
2 Wrap around the dog's muzzle with the knot under the lower jaw.

3 Tie firmly behind the dog's head.
Note: the susceptibilty of Boxers to airway compromise.

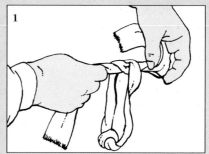

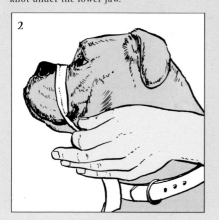

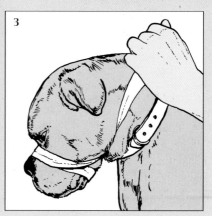

GLOSSARY

Angulation
The angles created by bones meeting at a joint.
Breed standard
The description laid down by the Kennel Club of the perfect breed specimen.
Brood bitch
A female dog which is used for breeding.
Carpals
These are the wrist bones.
Croup
This is the dog's rump: the front of the pelvis to the start of the tail.
Dam
The mother of puppies.

Dew claw
A fifth toe above the ground on the inside of the legs.
Elbow
The joint at the top of the forearm below the upper arm.
Flank
The area between the last rib and hip on the side of the body.
Furnishings
The long hair on the head, legs, thighs, back of buttocks or tail.
Gait
How a dog moves at different speeds.
Guard hairs
Long hairs that grow through the undercoat.
Muzzle
The foreface, or front of the head.

Occiput
The back upper part of the skull.
Oestrus
The periods when a bitch is 'on heat' or 'in season' and responsive to mating.
Pastern
Between the wrist (carpus) and the digits of the forelegs.
Scissor bite
Strong jaws with upper teeth overlapping lower ones.
Stifle
The hind leg joint, or 'knee'.
Undercoat
A dense, short coat hidden below the top-coat.
Whelping
The act of giving birth.
Whelps
Puppies that have not been weaned.
Whiskers
Long hairs on the jaw and muzzle.

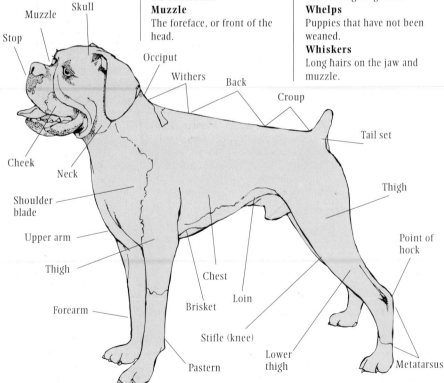

Muzzle
Skull
Stop
Occiput
Withers
Back
Croup
Tail set
Cheek
Neck
Shoulder blade
Upper arm
Thigh
Forearm
Thigh
Chest
Loin
Point of hock
Brisket
Stifle (knee)
Lower thigh
Metatarsus
Pastern

INDEX

USEFUL ADDRESSES

Animal Aunts
Wydnooch,
45 Fairview Road
Headley Down
Hampshire
GU38 8HQ
(Home sitters,
holidays)

**Animal Studies
Centre**
Waltham-on-the-Wolds
Melton Mowbray
Leics LE14 4RS
(Animal nutrition)

**Association of Pet
Behaviour
Counsellors**
257 Royal College
Street
London
NW1 9LU

**British Veterinary
Association**
7 Mansfield Street
London W1M 0AT

**Dog Breeders
Insurance Co Ltd**
9 St Stephens Court
St Stephens Road
Bournemouth BH2 6LG
(Books of cover notes
for dog breeders)

**Featherbed
Country Club,**
High Wycombe,
Bucks
(Luxury dog
accommodation)

**Guide Dogs for the
Blind Association**
Hillfield
Burghfield
Reading
RG7 3YG

**Hearing Dogs for
the Deaf**
The Training Centre
London Road
Lewknor
Oxon OX9 5RY

Home Sitters
Buckland Wharf
Buckland, Aylesbury
Bucks HP22 5LO

The Kennel Club
1-5 Clarges Street,
Piccadilly
London
W1Y 8AB
(Breed Standards,
Breed Club and Field
Trial contact
addresses, registration
forms, Good Citizen
training scheme)

**National Canine
Defence League**
1 & 2 Pratt Mews
London
NW1 0AD

**Pets As Therapy
(PAT Dogs)**
6 New Road, Ditton
Kent
ME20 6AD

(Information: how
friendly dogs can join
the hospital visiting
scheme)

**PRO Dogs National
Charity**
4 New Road, Ditton
Kent
ME20 6AD
(Information: Better
British Breeders,
worming certificates to
provide with puppies,
how to cope with grief
on the loss of a loved
dog etc.)

**Royal Society for
the Prevention of
Cruelty to Animals**
RSPCA Headquarters
Causeway
Horsham
West Sussex
RH12 1HG

SCAMPERS SCHOOL FOR DOGS

Scampers helps to train over 200 dogs and puppies every week, using kind, reward-based methods and behaviour therapy, in its unique indoor training facilities. Expert advice is given on all aspects of dog care, and there are puppy, beginners, intermediate and advanced classes. Scampers also run courses for other dog trainers and people interested in a career in dog training.

Scampers Pet Products
This specialist mail order service provides special products, including books, videos, toys, accessories and training equipment, for dog owners. It is based

at Scampers Petcare Superstore, which offers one of the largest ranges of dog accessories in the UK. For more information on Scampers School for Dogs, Scampers Petcare Superstore or Scampers Pet Products contact:

Scampers Petcare Superstore
Northfield Road
Soham
Nr. Ely
Cambs CB7 5UF
Tel: 01353 720431
Fax: 01353 624202